A READER'S GUIDE TO *THE DAY THE REVOLUTION BEGAN*

N.T. WRIGHT

AND THE REVOLUTIONARY CROSS

D E R E K   V R E E L A N D

N.T. Wright and the Revolutionary Cross: A Reader's Guide to
The Day the Revolution Began

Copyright © 2017 by Derek E. Vreeland
www.derekvreeland.com

Published by Doctrina Press

Printed in the United States of America

Cover and interior design by IndieDesignz.com

ISBN-13: 978-1973839415

ISBN-10: 1973839415

In this reader's guide Derek Vreeland leads us through one of Wright's most important works. Providing the necessary background, locating the central themes, and giving the theological history, he unfolds Wright's majestic treatment of the cross of Christ in a way readers can follow quickly. In so doing, this careful student of N.T. Wright has made it possible for the rest of us students to dive more deeply into what God has accomplished in Christ's death on a cross. I highly recommend *N.T. Wright and the Revolutionary Cross*.

> —DAVID FITCH, B.R. Lindner Chair of Evangelical Theology, Northern Seminary, author of *Faithful Presence*

Like a skilled explorer and careful guide, Derek Vreeland once again helps people climb Mount N.T. Wright. Within the pages of *N.T. Wright and the Revolutionary Cross*, Derek helps us see that the cross is so much more than we realize at first glance. This reader's guide is a great treasure chest that will bring to light the unsearchable riches of Christ.

> —DERWIN GRAY, Lead Pastor, Transformation Church, author of *The High Definition Leader*

Derek Vreeland is among the most attentive readers of N.T. Wright that I know. More importantly, he stands at the intersection of academic theology and pastoral ministry. To be conversant in the language of the academy and the vernacular of the pew is a skill that is critically important if the work of theology is going to feed the flock of Jesus. With *N.T. Wright and the Revolutionary Cross*, Derek Vreeland has made important developments in atonement theology accessible to the lay reader. As such, it is a timely and most welcome book!

> —BRIAN ZAHND, Lead Pastor, Word of Life Church, author of *Sinners in the Hands of a Loving God*

There are few theologians who are able to set crucial Christian doctrines within the grand sweep of the Bible's story like N.T. Wright. Yet it is easy to get lost or confused within a big and complex story. Even where there is a trail, it helps to have a guide. Derek Vreeland is the perfect guide into Wright's expansive work on the cross of Christ. A pastor and a scholar, Vreeland has not simply summarized Wright; he has translated him into our own context, making these vital truths come alive for us as pastors and as followers of Jesus the crucified and risen Lord.

—GLENN PACKIAM, Associate Senior Pastor, New Life Church, author of *Discover the Mystery of Faith*

Derek Vreeland brilliantly articulates and unpacks the theological genius of N.T. Wright. Vreeland offers a concise roadmap to *The Day the Revolution Began* in a way that is accessible for emerging theologians, pastors, and your everyday lay leader.

—TARA BETH LEACH, Senior Pastor, PazNaz, author of *Emboldened: A Vision for Empowering Women in Ministry*

Trust me, I love N.T. Wright. I love how he writes and why he writes, but adding Señor Vreeland into the mix allowed me to feel like I could actually navigate my way into this important conversation. Wright's book is like a long and beautiful road trip, and this reader's guide to *The Day the Revolution Began* is the GPS that helped me navigate the roads I could have easily gotten lost in. Thank you Derek for your co-piloting skills and for even taking the driver's seat when necessary. We all owe you some gas money.

—CARLOS A. RODRIGUEZ, founder, HappySonship.com, author of *Drop The Stones*

Derek Vreeland is a true student of N.T. Wright's prodigious body of work. He is also among Wright's finest interpreters and a serious Bible teacher in his own right. In this reader's guide to *The Day the Revolution Began*, Vreeland is a trustworthy guide and faithful companion. He has skillfully crafted questions that make Wright's atonement theology accessible to individuals or group studies, empowering readers in their own exploration and reflection. Best of all, his outline on the death of Christ through the pages of Romans is definitive. Bravo!

—BRAD JERSAK, author of *A More Christlike God*

Confused and overwhelmed by the brilliant, beautiful, but dense work of N.T. Wright? If so, Derek Vreeland's *N.T. Wright and the Revolutionary Cross* is just what you need to unpack Wright's *The Day The Revolution Began*. Without the impenetrable theological language, Vreeland translates Wright in words, images, and everyday theology that blesses every reader. Vreeland is your tour guide into one of today's most read and respected theologians.

—SEAN PALMER, Teaching Pastor, Ecclesia Houston, author of *Unarmed Empire*

CONTENTS

Preface

I have considered N.T. (Tom) Wright my professor for a number of years now. He has become my primary theological mentor. My theology and my pastoral ministry have been shaped by the theological vision given to us by Professor Wright. In 2015 I released a short summary of Tom's massive work on Paul's theology, *Paul and the Faithfulness of God*. My reader's guide, *Through the Eyes of N.T. Wright,* was an attempt to make accessible the key concepts in Tom's big book on Paul for those who might struggle to work through the book on their own. I would never have imagined the amount of positive feedback I received from people who found my little book so helpful. I am humbled by how well-received and widespread that book has become. When I first heard that Tom was working on a book on the death of Jesus, I was thrilled and thought another summary was in order.

I was pleased to have a brief conversation with him at Missio Alliance's Awakenings gathering in Alexandria, Virginia in April, 2017. He expressed appreciation for the summary work I did on *Paul and the Faithfulness of God* and said he understood my desire to continue to get his message out to a broader audience. In some ways this reader's guide is similar to the guide I wrote for the big book on

Paul. While in my previous reader's guide I did less interpretive work, I do more in this one. As I have become more familiar with Tom's work and as it has affected my own, I have grown more comfortable with blending my own interpretation of Tom with his key concepts. Another difference between this reader's guide and the last is I have included reflection questions at the end of each chapter to be used for personal or small group study.

Tom's much-awaited book on the cross arrived in the U.S. and the UK on October 12, 2016. Tom has become the rockstar theologian of our generation and so many of us theology nerds and N.T. Wright super-fans were waiting for this book like crazed music fans waiting for their favorite band to drop a new album. Luckily we did not have to camp outside a record store in some insane line to get our hands on this new book. Gone are those days. He publishes in the U.S. under the name "N.T. Wright" and publishes in the UK under the less formal name "Tom Wright." At times his books are published under different titles, which I find a bit confusing. The book on the cross has been published under the same title worldwide: *The Day the Revolution Began: Reconsidering the Meaning of Jesus's Crucifixion.*

People had been eagerly waiting for this book because both critics and fans of Tom felt a bit frustrated that he had not dedicated an entire volume to the complexities of the atonement. He had sparred with John Piper over the doctrine of justification in a well-known debate regarding Paul's use of the phrases "righteousness of God" and "justified by faith" in his book *Justification.* He has written a number of helpful books on the historical Jesus, books like *The Challenge of Jesus, Simply Jesus, How God Became King*, and his scholarly work, *Jesus and the Victory of God.* He touched on the meaning of the gospel in *Simply Good News* where he made a few passing remarks on the atonement, but he had not addressed the topic of the meaning of the cross until this book.

This reader's guide is not intended to be read in place of Tom's book. There is no way I can capture all the nuance in a summary work like this one. Any missing details or supporting bits of evidence in my work are the result of difficult editorial choices and should not reflect poorly on the very complex concepts in Tom's book. Furthermore if you want to know whether what I have written is what Tom said or is what I am saying, you will have to read my book alongside *The Day the Revolution Began*. I quote from Tom's book sparingly but when I use a direct quote I cite the page number within parentheses after the quotation like this: (Wright, 12). Also work through this reader's guide with a Bible close by. I quote from the *English Standard Version* (ESV) but at times I only include Scripture references and not the complete text. It would be helpful to read those passages mentioned in this reader's guide so you are not lost.

I share Tom's desire for readers to work towards the meaning of the cross, which means we will not only be learning new things about what the cross means for followers of Jesus, but we will also need to unlearn some things. Learning is difficult enough, but the real work of renewing our minds in Christ is in the unlearning. The subtitle of the book tips us off right away that we will need to do some unlearning as we will be reconsidering the meaning of the cross. To "reconsider" implies that we have already thought about the cross and our thinking up to this point may not be sufficient. The message in the subtitle does not imply that the Church has got the cross completely wrong up to this point and that now Tom is going to put us on the right path. No way! Rather the task of reconsidering the meaning of the cross implies that we have some faulty assumptions in how we have viewed the cross, and these faulty assumptions have left us with a limited view. I appreciate Tom's respect for the broad Christian tradition in general and the Reformed tradition specifically. As a Bishop in the Anglican Communion, Tom remains respectful of the past work on the atonement within the Reformed tradition even when he critiques parts of it. As we work towards reconsidering what the cross means, we discover more than we ever would have imagined.

I want to help readers probe Tom's book for the deep meaning contained there so we can together discover and rediscover the cross in all of its wonder, beauty, and saving power. Tom is not only a brilliant theologian; he is also a warm and colorful writer, which is a rare combination for a Bible scholar. *The Day the Revolution Began* is a book of theology, and "theology" is not a bad word. We do not need to feel intimidated by theology, because it isn't just the work of academic types tucked away behind piles of dusty old books in poorly lit corners of seminary libraries. Christian theology is a conversation. It is how we in the Church talk about God based on what we think about God. It's a critical conversation as the God we believe in and worship shapes both the people we are becoming and the world where we live.

Christian theology is a 2,000 year-old conversation among preachers and prophets, scholars and shoemakers. Theology is not the study of God as much as it is a study of how God has chosen to reveal himself. God has revealed himself in creation, in Scripture, in the sacraments, in prayer, in the long winding story of the Great Tradition and the broad history of the Church. God has revealed himself supremely in sending his Son. Never is the focus of God's revelation more clear than when Jesus is suffering on the cross. This conversation has been ongoing throughout the history of the Church and has taken many twists and turns along the way. Each era of Christian history has value and adds particular comments to the conversation, but each generation must wrestle with the Bible anew to see if we have new insights to bring to the ancient conversation. Theology is not reserved for intellectuals, although we welcome and value their contribution; theology is a whole-people-of-God activity. Tom has been an advocate for this approach throughout his career as a bishop and professor which has allowed him to have one foot in the Church and one foot in the academy. This book typifies that bridge between the tools of rigorously scholastic biblical research and the life of the local church.

The Day the Revolution Began is a book on the atonement, a discussion on how the death of Jesus saves us from our sins. In the Nicene Creed we confess "for us and for our salvation he came down from heaven...for our sake he was crucified under Pontius Pilate." As Christians we all believe "Christ died for our sins" (1 Corinthians 15:3). Nevertheless, the Church has never corporately and definitively pinned down a theological explanation concerning precisely *how* the death of Jesus saves us. Throughout history Christians have constructed theories to explain how the death of Jesus atones for our sin. These theories are not the gospel. They are all attempts to work with the Scripture in order to explore the full meaning of Jesus' death. Some of the better known atonement theories include:

- Recapitulation Theory: Jesus comes to sum up the entire life of Adam including taking Adam's sin and experience of death to become the head of a new humanity.
- Ransom Theory: Jesus' death is a payment made for the debt incurred by sin.
- Moral Influence Theory: Jesus dies as a sacrifice for sin, setting an example for us to follow.
- Christus Victor: Jesus' death sets us free from the power of sin and the satan.
- Satisfaction Theory: Jesus' death satisfies God's demands for justice and honor.
- Propitiation Theory: Jesus' death turns away the wrath of God.
- Penal Substitution Theory: Jesus dies in the place of sinners taking upon himself the penalty sinners deserve.

Tom has tended to avoid speculative atonement theories which try to explain too much, choosing rather to allow the biblical writers to describe the implications of the death of Jesus in narrative form as they work with the big story the Bible is telling. The purpose of this reader's guide is to offer you a roadmap through Tom's book, to bring to the surface the key themes and conclusions he draws. I hope to stir your thinking, prompt new conversations about the cross, cause your love for Christ to grow, and equip the Church to carry forth her gospel-shaped mission.

I am thankful for the small group that met at my church, Word of Life Church in St. Joseph, Missouri, on Sunday nights during Lent in March and April 2017 to study and discuss the themes in Tom's book. I appreciate their willingness to attend what turned into a theological lecture with Q&A and roundtable discussions. Their questions and input have shaped my reader's guide. Thank you Steve Michael, Merle Stowell, Chris Sargent, Jay Summers, Jason Burkeybile, Debbie & Paul Kunz, Carolyn Hubach, Ellen Sybert, Leisa Blair, Susan Whitman, Sherri Evans, Pam Keefer, Dan & Marianne Brachman, and Andrew Kar.

I also deeply appreciate all of the careful editing by my friend Janene Collins. She took the time to proofread each week's lecture notes for our Sunday night small group, notes that were also posted on my blog, notes which became the framework for this book. Thanks also to my friends, Peri Zahnd and Marilyn Bischoff, for taking the time to read over my manuscript. Their attention to detail has made my writing better. I am deeply grateful for the support of my wife Jenni who gives me the time and space to teach and write on theological themes that have so captured my imagination.

Thanks also to my pastor, Brian Zahnd, for the many, many conversations about Tom's work and for the encouragement to continue to write and do the work of theology as a part of my pastoral vocation. And finally thanks to Professor Wright for taking the time to review this reader's guide. Your attentive eye and helpful comments allowed me to sharpen my summary and interpretation of your book. I so deeply appreciate your theological work for the Church. Thank you for challenging us and inspiring us to think Christianly as the people of God's new creation.

My prayer is that this little book will continue to equip the Church for her mission to make cross-shaped disciples throughout all the world.

Keep, O Lord, your household the Church in your steadfast faith and love, that through your grace we may proclaim your truth with boldness, and minister your justice with compassion; for the sake of our Savior Jesus Christ, who lives and reigns with you and the Holy Spirit, one God, now and for ever. Amen.

Derek Vreeland
Second Sunday after Pentecost 2017

GETTING THINGS STARTED

The Day the Revolution Began,
Chapters 1-3

Wright opens the book with a telling of the death of Jesus in story form. Such an opening is a sign of things to come. He emphasizes the narrative nature of the gospel in the context of the larger story the Scripture tells. In the opening paragraph he imagines the death of Jesus in its historical setting without much fanfare. Rome has executed another political rival because this is what Rome does. But death is not the end of the Jesus story. As followers of Jesus look back at the cross through the resurrection they see that a revolution was launched when Jesus died.

The resurrection completely changes how we see the cross. Instead of reflecting on the cross as a sad, pitiful end to another Jewish revolutionary, we see the cross as the beginning of a worldwide revolution. Today we often assume Jesus died so we could go to heaven when we die; the early Christians talked about the death of Jesus in ways that were bigger, more subversive, and downright revolutionary. Wright has been criticized for not emphasizing the personal implications of salvation including the hope of heaven, so he makes a clear statement in the beginning of Chapter 1 that the personal meaning of the cross as related to an individual's forgiveness and assurance of heaven is not forsaken in this more revolutionary view of the cross. Personal forgiveness and the experience of heaven upon death are included in Wright's view, but we can no longer go on talking about going to heaven when we die as we have in the past. These experiences are themselves short chapters in a much larger story of creation and new creation.

We can find agreement and a common confession with the Apostle Paul when he writes, "...the life I now live in the flesh I live by faith in the Son of God, who loved me and gave himself for me" (Galatians 2:20). Praise directed to God rises in our hearts when we think about the great expression of love displayed in the death of Jesus for each of us individually. However, if we limit the meaning of the cross to simply the personal benefits we receive, we run the risk of reducing the faith to a private and ultimately self-focused experience. A bigger view of the cross reveals that the death of Jesus makes an incredible difference not just for individuals but for the entire world, which prompts the "why" questions. *Why is the cross so powerful? Why does the cross continue to captivate our imaginations? Why does the death of Christ continue to change the lives of millions?*

Wright tells the story of an unnamed Roman Catholic archbishop who tells a story of three troublesome boys who continually played jokes on the priest at their local parish. When the priest confronted the boys, two ran off, but he stopped one of them. He instructed the boy to stand in front of the crucifix and say out loud to Jesus three times, "You did all that for me, and I don't give that much" (Wright, 12). (The boy was instructed to snap his fingers the second time he said "that.") The boy did it twice, but on his third attempt he broke down crying. The archbishop who tells the story said he was that boy who that day became completely overcome by the cross. According to Wright, "You don't have to have a theory about why the cross is so powerful before you can be moved and changed, before you can know yourself loved and forgiven, because of Jesus's death" (Wright, 12). A person may be as unassuming as a mischievous boy in a local parish and still be moved by the power of the cross.

While exploring the meaning of the cross is a worthwhile endeavor, it isn't necessary to be able to articulate with theological depth the implications of the cross in order to encounter Jesus and enter into the kingdom of God. We don't have to fully understand the cross any more than we need to explain how the elements of communion connect us with Jesus; we just need to be present in humility and faith. Many of the great hymns and prayers of the Church help us encounter the reality of the living Christ and experience the love of God through the death of Jesus. We are well served to pause and stand in awe of the beauty and the mystery of Christ, but Wright argues it is vital to our faith to search out the meaning of the cross, to seek to answer the "why" questions as we worship the crucified Christ.

Asking ourselves why Jesus died includes two different sets of questions. First, we have to ask historical questions, asking why Jewish leaders and the Roman governor wanted to execute Jesus. Second, we have to ask theological questions of which there are many. As Wright has advised in other works, it is critical that we answer the big questions by marrying together the historical questions with the theological questions. The strength of Wright's approach to understanding the death of Jesus is rooted in his desire to bridge the gap between history and theology. History, the record of what has occurred in the past, and theology, the ongoing conversation about what we think and say about God, are natural partners. Wright's preaching, teaching, lecturing, and writing have reverberated with this theme: history and theology go together hand in hand.

Holy and inspired Scripture is the table where all Christian theology comes to sit, and biblical theology focuses specifically on how the writers of the Bible spoke about God and God's work in the world. Without reading the biblical writers in their historical context, it is too easy to misunderstand biblical texts by allowing modern cultural perspectives to reshape texts into what we want them to say, instead of allowing them to speak on their own. One classic and common error in biblical interpretation is importing a modern concept or theme into a specific Bible passage. We do want to understand what the Bible means for us today, but before we can understand what it *means* we have to work hard to understand what it *meant* at the time it was written.

Asking the Right Questions

Asking ourselves "Why did Jesus die?" first prompts historical questions: *Why did Jewish leaders and the Roman governor want to execute Jesus?* This is followed by theological questions: *What does the death of Jesus reveal about God? What did the death of Jesus accomplish? How did this awful implement of torture and death become the enduring symbol of a worldwide movement?* Roman crucifixion was so shameful that it wasn't talked about openly in the first century world. Early followers of Jesus could have brushed over the cross and focused solely on the resurrection of Jesus in order to avoid the ridicule and confusion, but they did just the opposite. They followed the lead of the Apostle Paul who wrote: "For I decided to know nothing among you except Jesus Christ and him crucified" (1 Corinthians 2:2). Early Christians celebrated the cross, but they did not define it.

Modern Christians have the opportunity to grow in their understanding of the cross because we have two thousand years of reflection on it, but we don't start with the theological puzzles created by theologians over the years. Rather, we start by looking at the crucifixion of Jesus within the context of the big story the Bible is telling. When we step back from the discussions and debates about atonement theories and take a look at the death of Jesus inside the big story the Bible is telling, then with fresh eyes we can make sense of some of the theological puzzles created by various atonement theories. *What did the biblical writers and the early Christians mean when they wrote about Jesus dying for our sins?*

During the first four hundred years of Christian reflection, we find no clear, universally recognized statement on the exact meaning of the cross. We don't find finely tuned conversations on the cross in the same way Christians talked with precision about the human and divine nature of Jesus and the fantastic mystery of the Trinity. Early Christians, like the biblical writers, used various metaphors to describe the cross, but the Church adopted no credal statement defining with specificity how the cross saves us. The important early creeds of the Church did not contain what we now know as atonement theories. However, three recurring themes regarding the cross can be found in the writings of the early church fathers: (1) Through the cross God secured victory over the powers of evil. (2) Jesus died in our place so we do not, in one sense, need to experience death. (3) Jesus' death was sacrificial.

These themes did not exist as stand-alone theories, but as metaphors within the story the Bible tells. For early Christians it was not necessary to specify a particular explanation of exactly *how* the death of Jesus saves. Many of the current debates surrounding the meaning of the crucifixion are rooted in the Protestant

Reformation of the sixteenth century. The Reformers did not devote as much attention to the future of God's people as they did to the salvation of God's people, which is problematic. Understanding the implications of salvation, what we are saved *for*, is crucial in understanding how the cross saves. If what we are headed for is spiritual union with God in a disembodied heaven, where our spiritual feet will walk on streets of gold forever, then what we need to be saved from are those things that would prevent us from experiencing this heavenly bliss. However, if what we are being saved for is more than going to heaven when we die (and it is!), then what we are being saved *from* and what Jesus saves us *for* are altogether different. The Reformation was, in part, a response to two doctrines within Roman Catholicism: purgatory and the Mass. Refuting these two doctrines had a direct effect on how the Reformers talked about the cross. The questions the Reformers were asking shaped the answers they found in the cross.

The Reformers and Their Questions

During medieval Catholicism, purgatory developed as the belief in a place of temporary punishment whereby Christians could suffer, fully paying satisfaction to God for their sins before going to heaven. The Reformers opposed this teaching. Behind this doctrine was the emphasis within Roman Catholicism on heaven or hell as the final destination of the human soul. Absent from their view of the future was the biblical emphasis on new creation. Heaven was the goal, not the reconciliation of heaven and earth. The Reformers argued that purgatory was unnecessary. Christians didn't need to suffer after they died in order to be purified from their sins and enter heaven because, according to their interpretation of the cross, Jesus was punished for sinners on the cross. In this regard Jesus not only bore our sins on the cross but also the wrath of God against sins. Since Jesus was punished in our place, there was no need for Christians to be punished temporarily in purgatory. The connection between a refutation of the need to "make satisfaction to God" through penance and purgatory and the necessity of Jesus satisfying the wrath of God can be found in Calvin's *Institutes of the Christian Religion* 3.4.25-26.

The particular point of opposition for the Reformers in their critique of the celebration of the Mass was the Roman Catholic understanding that, in one sense, the priest was sacrificing Jesus again in order to make atonement for sins. The Reformers again looked to their understanding of the cross to point out the impossibility of sacrificing and re-sacrificing Jesus at every Mass. According to the Reformers, Jesus suffered on the cross in our place once for all. They pointed to the "finished worked of Christ" upon the cross where he suffered punishment in our place. Our justification was made secure by Jesus' death alone without the need for any further works, like the work of the priest during Mass. As with purgatory, the Reformers drew upon penal substitutionary atonement to form their argument against the Mass and their interpretation of justification by works. What they missed was questioning the assumption of divine wrath and the need somehow for that wrath to be pacified.

The Reformers provided correct answers. They were just asking the wrong questions. We are indeed justified by faith and not by works, but the problem was not that we required justification because God was angry and his justice required his anger to be satisfied. The question we need to ask in light of the big story of Scripture is not: *What is necessary for individuals to escape the wrathful punishment of God?* The right question in light of Scripture is: *What is necessary for us to participate in God's work of redeeming and restoring the world?* The right answers about justification to the wrong questions about pacifying an angry god mixed with a limited vision of the future has created what Wright calls a "paganized vision" of the cross, a vision not consistent with the early Christians. We will look at this topic in more detail in Chapter 3.

For Wright, atonement is connected to eschatology. The meaning of the death of Jesus is connected to how we understand "end things." Eschatology is the study of the end—that is, the end of our lives, the end of the world, and the end of this present age. Justification is a present pronouncement concerning a future event. God declares that all who believe in the crucified and risen Jesus are in the right, in the covenant, and therefore justified participants in God's new creation. The Reformers remained fixed on an eschatology of going to heaven or hell shaping their interpretation of justification in terms of being right with God so that individuals could go to heaven and miss the punishment of hell. In retrospect, they would have seen a broader view of the end, which includes new creation, had they emphasized Ephesians in the same way they emphasized Romans and Galatians. Ephesians 1:10 describes this broader view to include God's purpose "to unite all things in him, things in heaven and things on earth." This view includes the remaking and ultimate marriage of heaven and earth, whereby God's space and humanity's space are permanently joined together that God may dwell in his creation with his people forever.

What we believe about how the cross saves (atonement) is connected to what we believe about how things end (eschatology). Working towards an understanding of atonement that is consistent with the vision of the New Testament writers and the early Christians requires a biblical vision of the end. Wright has helped us rethink our eschatology in many of his works including the popular *Surprised By Hope* and his large academic work on Paul's theology, *Paul and the Faithfulness of God.* His book on the cross follows the implications of our rethought eschatology. If the end is not enjoying God forever in a disembodied heaven and is instead bodily resurrection and new creation, then maybe the death of Christ is not a matter of appeasing an angry God so we can go to heaven when we die. Wright helps us rethink atonement with words like these, "The cross was the moment when something *happened* as a result of which the world became a different place, inaugurating God's future plan. The revolution began then and there; Jesus' resurrection was the first sign that it was indeed underway" (Wright, 34).

The mistakes made by the Reformers were compounded by the influence of the Enlightenment on Protestant churches with an exaggerated emphasis on the individual. The popular assumption in Protestant Europe and the United States in the 1800s had become: Jesus died for *my* sins to take *me* to heaven when *I* die and because of *my* sin *I* am under the wrath of God. Thankfully *my* Savior died for *me*, saving *me* from *my* sin and the wrath of God. The problem with this heightened view on the individual was the division it created between personal sins and systemic sins, the big systems of evil in the world.

Popular atonement theologies during this time saw the cross as the remedy for our personal sins while societal problems and global evil had to be dealt with by means other than a deep reflection on the cross. This thinking fed into the pervasive secularism deeply imbedded within the Enlightenment, where religion found a home in the private lives of Christians, but had little to say about global and political problems. American Christianity by the 1900s found much energy in evangelicalism whereby the cross became the centerpiece of saving souls for heaven. By the time of the second World War, the cross had been stripped of all its revolutionary power to fuel the breaking in of new creation into our broken-down world. This poor way of thinking continues into modern times. For example, the popular reaction to the September 11 terrorist attacks was to call it "evil" and then go drop bombs, as if dropping bombs would somehow rid the world of evil. When we begin to see the cross as revolutionary, we begin to see the truth that the cross is how God has dealt with evil, all evil.

The Gospel in Modern Ears

The most popular gospel "formula" for modern American evangelicals is one that goes something like this: *You have sinned. Sin separates you from God. Jesus died for your sins to bridge the gap. Accept Jesus as your personal Lord and Savior so you can have a personal relationship with God and go to heaven when you die.* This formula is not altogether untrue, but neither is it what we find in the New Testament, at least not the New Testament read in the context of the history of the first-century Jewish and Roman worlds. This shrunken view of the gospel has no power to confront evil.

The problem with the popular American evangelical formula is that it completely ignores the story of Israel, as if God's dealing with Israel and most importantly God's covenant with Abraham has no relevance to the story of Jesus. I remember entering into seminary a bit embarrassed that my working knowledge of the Old Testament was so weak. Growing up in American evangelicalism, particularly of the Pentecostal/charismatic variety, formed me in a way to overlook the old covenant in favor of the new covenant, a better covenant based on "better promises" (Hebrews 8:6). In one sense the old covenant has become obsolete, but there is no way to understand the intricacies of the new covenant without understanding the nature of the old one. I am now convinced that removing the death of Jesus from its historic and particularly Jewish setting is the fastest way to shipwreck our faith in the shallow waters of individualistic biblical principles. The cross viewed from the perspective of the Jewish and Roman worlds expands our faith whereby we can see the overthrow of the powers of empire. This kind of faith is a faith that has something to say to the real world about real world problems. A historically grounded view of the cross enables us to see God's solution not only for personal sins, but systemic sins energized by the idols of secularism, individualism, and nationalism.

Some people hear the gospel as the answer to the problem, not of evil, but of an angry God. I do not know of any theologian who would state it quite like this, but sadly some Christians seem focused on an angry God who stands ready to pour out retributive wrath on them. They think God is love, but he's also angry. The good news they hear is that Jesus satisfied the wrath of God for us. This version of the gospel leaves many with the impression that God is not pure love, but a god mixed with love and wrath. Unfortunately, some people reject the Christian faith over this misunderstanding of the gospel. Others reread the Scriptures and the early church fathers to discover God is always and only love; the cross reveals the co-suffering, self-giving love of God who has defeated the powers of sin, death, and hell. The death of Jesus and his subsequent resurrection form the climax of the story of God's kingdom of heaven coming to earth, the story of the God of Israel renewing the covenant, forgiving sins, and bringing an end to the exile of God's people. This is the story the Bible is telling.

The vision of a "holy" god who justifiably requires violence in order to save has been called into question by many who have looked with horror and disgust at a world at war. Questioning the necessity of violence and punishment in considering the meaning of the cross has raised a number of questions: *Does the God and Father of Jesus use violence for his purposes? Does the Father use violence against the Son? What about divine punishment? Does God use violence to punish people?* We see both punishment and violence in the Bible, but the Church offers a number of different ways to interpret divine punishment. One way is to say that God hates sins and punishes sinners, but luckily for us Jesus has stepped in and taken the punishment God intended for us. Some Christians interpret divine punishment like this, but *is this the consistent picture of God we see throughout the entire story of Scripture? Is this the God we see revealed supremely in Jesus?* Again while no respected theologian or preacher would say it like this, some people in the pew hear the gospel sounding something like: "God so hated the world, that he killed his only son" (Wright, 43). This rewriting of John 3:16 is the very distortion we end up with if our view of God is one of an angry deity hell-bent on violent punishment.

The story of a "holy" angry god sounds like human bullies who use their power to intimidate and threaten to get their way. If God required his anger to be appeased and we want to call that "love," then many people will gladly say, "No thank you. I don't want anything to do with that God." This interpretation is only one of the ways to talk about how the death of Jesus is connected to punishment. There are better and more biblical ways to talk about the punishment of sin, which we will discover as we look at the Scripture with fresh eyes. Some Christians will argue that if God is willing to employ violence to accomplish his saving, forgiving, work then we human beings have an example to follow. We too can justify violence if our anger is "righteous." How Christians talk about issues like global terrorism and capital punishment is rooted in our views of the atonement. *If we are to reject the view that depicts a wrathful God using violence to pacify God's own anger in the death of Jesus, then what are the alternatives?*

First, the death of Jesus wins a decisive victory over the "powers" of this dark and evil age dominated by sin and death. This view raises a number of questions that we will explore in later chapters. Second, the death of Christ reveals the love of God in a unique and powerful way so that it becomes an example for us to follow. However, this view also raises questions, primarily: *How does Jesus' death necessarily reveal the love of God?* I could try to prove to my wife that I love her by jumping into a freezing cold lake in the middle of winter, but that doesn't demonstrate love or courage unless jumping into the lake was in some way necessary, if for example my wife was drowning in the middle of that lake. However if she was not drowning and there was no reason for jumping into an icy lake in winter, my action would demonstrate my foolishness, not my love. If the death of Jesus achieved something that could have been achieved many other ways, then the particular death of Jesus neither demonstrates God's love nor provides an example to follow.

Jesus' death on the cross was not accidental. Jesus died for a distinct purpose. *What was that purpose?* This is the question Wright will pursue throughout the rest of the book. This pursuit has led to a variety of different discussions regarding Christian nonviolence, the Trinity, the relationship between the Father and the Son, the incarnation, and the nature of God. Wright does not discuss all of these issues in depth, but grounds our discussion of the meaning of the death of Jesus in an eschatology shaped by the story of new creation, the story of Scripture itself.

A Historical Point of View

History matters. We understand the various meanings of the cross when we seek to understand them in the historical context of the writers of the New Testament. A wide-angle view of the history surrounding the crucifixion begins with a look at the world of the Roman Empire built on top of an older Greek culture. Homer's epic poem *The Iliad* is all about wrath, the vengeance of the Greeks. It opens with a reference to wrath. Virgil, the Roman counterpart to Homer, opens his epic poem with a nod towards weapons of combat. These two classic works of Greek and Roman literature dealing with the subjects of war and violence provide some of the backdrop to the crucifixion. While followers of the crucified Christ see wrath and arms, war and battle differently, this world of violence helps modern-day readers understand why a Jewish prophet proclaiming the kingdom of God at the beginning of the first century would be killed in such a cruel and merciless way.

Crucifixion was perfected by the Roman Empire as a way to execute rebels, traitors, slaves, and violent criminals in public view to remind people of the might and sovereignty of the empire. Romans and Jews alike viewed crucifixion as abhorrent and a public humiliation, too ghastly to talk about in public. Crucifixion had both political and cultural meanings which help us understand the cross theologically. Victims dying on a Roman cross died slow agonizing deaths, adding unspeakable shame to their pain. While Rome did not invent this form of public execution, they experimented with forms of crucifixion in order to assert Roman dominance over all political rivals. Jesus, according to Wright, "grew up under the shadow of the cross" (Wright, 57). Jewish revolts had sprung up in the days before Jesus, and Rome had crushed them every time. Jesus grew up hearing the stories and seeing the horror of Roman crosses. As Jesus was proclaiming the kingdom of God, his Jewish audience would have known of Jewish rebels who had been executed by Roman officials. When people of Jesus' day heard anyone talk about "the cross," they knew all too well the shameful cruelty of it.

This historical account of crucifixion stands in the background of how early Christians understood the meaning of the cross. Their view of the cross was loaded with social, political, and religious meanings, all surrounding the might of the Roman Empire. The question for readers of the New Testament is: *How did the cross acquire such a fundamentally different meaning by the followers of Jesus?* Wright leads us into a discovery of the meaning of crucifixion from the perspective of the earliest Christians which will underscore the biblical and revolutionary roots of the cross in early Christian thought.

The ancient world of Greece and Rome was filled with stories of people who were sacrificed, or sacrificed themselves, to secure blessings or turn away divine wrath. These stories are almost never found in the Hebrew Scriptures. As Jewish leaders were plotting Jesus' death, Caiaphas argued that it was better that one man die for the people so the nation might be spared. According to Wright, this view is replete in pagan literature, where those who died on behalf of other people were considered to be dying an honorable sacrificial death. No one living in the Roman Empire would have called death by crucifixion "honorable." For Christians to speak of the death of Jesus upon the cross with any kind of significance would have been brushed off by Roman citizens as pure foolishness.

The Jewish World of the First Century

Within the wider cultural context of the Greco-Roman world, Wright looks with a more narrow focus on the Jewish world of the first century and offers three important considerations.

First, no Jewish festival was more important than the Passover, the commemoration of the time when the God of Israel delivered the people of Israel from Egyptian slavery. When Jesus chose to reveal the meaning of his death in the clearest terms, he did so at Passover during his final meal with his disciples just before his arrest. The Passover event became the primary way for early Christians to work towards understanding the implications of the death of Jesus.

Second, Jewish people of Jesus' day still saw themselves as exiles. While living in their homeland, they were still under the yoke of a foreign, pagan, occupying force. The Babylonian exile of more than five centuries had been extended into the present day. According to the prophet Jeremiah, God promised to do a new thing—to make a new covenant where sins would be forgiven, bringing their exile to an end. Daniel 9 also speaks of a coming day of renewal when sin will be put away with and the people of God will be restored.

Third, while many first-century Jews expected God's Messiah, God's reigning King, to come to enact this new covenant, none of them expected Messiah to come in the way Jesus did. They looked for Messiah to come to restore the kingdom to Israel, but none expected Messiah to suffer in the way Jesus did. In other words, they didn't have the complex understanding of the death of Messiah that the early Christians had. The Messiah was expected to be a conquering King, not a crucified one. They had no conceptual framework to match the intense suffering of crucifixion with the reign of Messiah. While the early Christians proclaimed Jesus as King who was crucified and raised, the first-century Jewish world shook their heads. For them, a crucified Messiah was a failed Messiah.

Wright will dedicate a large portion of the book to how early Christians read the Old Testament in light of the death, burial, and resurrection of Jesus, but he offers a few observations regarding the specific world of the first-century Christians. This world existed within a Jewish world, within the world of the Roman Empire. Wright describes early Christian reflections on the death of Jesus as the turning of a kaleidoscope, very familiar colors and shapes that have been configured in a new way. The themes of the New Testament writers included metaphors from the Jewish world in new and surprising ways. Wright will show how the themes work together later in the book. The Gospels (Matthew, Mark, Luke, and John) fit together with the Epistles (the letters of Paul, Peter, John, and others) in a cohesive way under the banner of the early Christian confession: "The Messiah died for our sins in accordance with the Bible," (1 Corinthians 15:3, Wright's translation). Early Christians interpreted "in accordance with the Bible" not as a few select verses in the Old Testament pointing to the death of Jesus, but as the entirety of the Old Testament, the law and the prophets, pointing to the death, resurrection, and reign of Messiah.

How do we see the meaning of the cross work out in the diversity of writing and writers in the New Testament? Wright sketches out his plan to answer that question with these points:

1. We need to reject the popular view of going to heaven when we die as the sole purpose of salvation, and replace it with the more biblical view of the new heavens and new earth at the end of the age.
2. Sin isn't what prevents us from going to heaven, but it is sin and the idolatry standing behind it that keep us from bearing the image of God in and for the world.
3. Idols have been empowered by human sin. When we participate in idolatry we give power to idols, a power that should be ours, a power they should never have had. For God's new creation to break in and renew the old broken-down creation, the power of idolatry must be broken.
4. God's act of dethroning the power of idols is God's way of dealing with sin so that human beings can be restored to God's image-bearers and thus fulfill their primary vocation.
5. God's single plan of dealing with the human plight, sin, corruption, and idolatry is centered in the story of Israel.
6. Jesus comes as Israel's Messiah and Israel's representative to do for Israel, and ultimately for the world, what Israel could not do for herself.
7. The climactic act of Jesus' death enacts God's revolutionary plan to rescue the world God loves.

Wright does not prefer the traditional word "atonement," and chooses to use it sparingly throughout the book. He does note that the English word "atonement" appears often in English translations of the Bible, but it means different things in different settings. It does not simply mean "what Jesus achieved on the cross" (Wright, 69). The New Testament in various places extends what Jesus has done for us and the world to the entire work of Jesus, not just his death. Furthermore, John's Revelation speaks of the Lamb slain from the foundation of the world. The idea of "atonement" reaches forward to the ascension of Jesus and reaches backwards to the foundation of human civilization.

Chapter 1 Reflection Questions

1. How would you describe your earliest encounter with the message of the cross? Was it one of awe, fear, love, or devotion?

2. What value is there in becoming aware of the history of the Church?

3. In what ways is our understanding of the end (eschatology) connected to our understanding of the meaning of the cross (atonement)?

4. Do you now or have you ever had a vision of an angry god who determined to punish you for your wrongdoing? Where do you think that image came from?

5. How do things change if you begin to see salvation in terms of what God is doing in and for the world more than simply what God is doing for you?

6. What are the differences in how people hear: "God so hated the world that he killed his only son" and "God so loved the world that he gave his only son"?

7. Why do you think Jesus waited until the Passover (the Last Supper) with his disciples to speak so clearly about his pending death?

8. Why do you think so many Jewish people did not expect the Messiah to come the way Jesus did?

THE STORIES OF ISRAEL

The Day the Revolution Began, Chapters 4-7

Many popular atonement theories have made the mistake of making heaven the goal of salvation, while the story of Scripture points us to the remaking of heaven and earth as God's ultimate goal. Equally problematic with some approaches to atonement is the misdiagnosis of the problem, the wrong assumption that the prevalence of sin implies that human beings have done wrong and thus need to be punished. Wright describes these mistakes as a "platonized goal" (*going to a disembodied heaven*) and a "moralizing diagnosis" (*the problem is that human beings have not kept the rules God commanded*), which together lead to a "paganized solution"

(*Jesus' death pacifies the anger of God*), a trifold mistake (Wright, 74). We will explore this problem in more detail in the next chapter.

With the goal of new creation in mind, we see that the primary problem is not merely that human beings have failed to obey God's moral commands, although that is a part of it. The primary problem for which human beings need rescue is idolatry and the corruptive forces unleashed on the earth when human beings reject the worship of the one true God and begin to worship idols. Wright calls the mistaken view the "works contract" whereby humanity is under contract with God to keep a certain code of moral behavior. Either humanity obeyed and was rewarded or they disobeyed and were punished. The good news for humanity, according to the works contract, was that Jesus obeyed God's rules according to the contract and took the punishment for disobedience that humanity deserved for not obeying God's rules.

For those who believe in Jesus according to the works contract, "righteousness" was transferred from Jesus to believers. "Righteousness" from this perspective is a moral status, like five gold stars, that has been conferred from Jesus to those who believe in him.

The problem with the works contract is that it is a shrunken view of the story the Bible tells. The works contract view ignores the heart of the Old Testament and oversimplifies the problem of human sin. The story the Bible tells about God's creation, humanity's purpose and failure, and God's solution in Christ is what Wright calls a "covenant of vocation." This vocation, or job given to humanity by God, was to reflect God's image into creation and echo all of creation's praise back to God the Creator. As a royal priesthood the people of God were to lead the way, demonstrating how human beings are to live in right relationship to God, creation, and one another. Disobedience lies at the surface of a deeper, more devastating issue—idolatry. When we fail to obey God's commands, we not only break God's laws, we empower dark forces through our idolatry that end up enslaving us and all creation. The solution needed to correct this problem is not that we need to be punished, but that these enslaving forces need to be broken.

The book of Revelation not only reveals this vocation to be kings and priests (Revelation 5:10) but also paints a picture of the end of our story, the great goal of God's rescuing work. This is not merely rescuing people from hell so they can go to heaven; rather God's goal is a coming together of heaven and earth. In this act of final reconciliation, God restores humanity's priestly vocation, free from idolatry and sin. Idolatry does not embolden God's desire to punish; idolatry corrupts the primary human vocation whereby we improperly live out our humanity. We not only fail to rule effectively in our royal position; idolatry corrupts our ability to live as adequate priests standing between heaven and earth. According to Wright, "We humans are called to stand at the intersection of heaven and earth, holding together in our hearts, our praises, and our urgent intercessions the loving wisdom of the Creator God and the terrible torments of his battered world" (Wright, 80).

One place where we see God's persistence in the viability of his covenant of vocation is 2 Corinthians 5:21, which is obscured by the works contract. Wright translates it like this: "*The Messiah did not know sin, but God made him to be sin on our behalf, so that in him we might embody God's faithfulness to the covenant*" (Wright, 81). The context of 2 Corinthians 5:21 is not "going to heaven when we die," but new creation and reconciliation (2 Corinthians 5:17).

Part of why Jesus saves us is so God's redeemed people can become the place where God's promises to Abraham are extended to the world. According to Galatians 3:13-14, the Messiah's death doesn't save people from hell but saves those under the law from the curse of the law so that the blessing of Abraham might come upon all the nations of the world. In his death Jesus is obedient not in the context of a works contract but, according to Romans 5:17, in the context of a priestly vocation. The death of Jesus restores us to our original vocation of being God's image-bearing caretakers of God's world. Sin implies a failure of that vocation. Idolatry, lying at the root of sin, represents humanity's fundamental rejection of that vocation.

A helpful way to think of death associated with human sin in the context of a covenant of vocation rather than in the context of a works contract is to think about the difference between getting a speeding ticket and experiencing a car wreck. If you speed you could get pulled over and get a ticket as a form of punishment. Or you could speed and end up in a car wreck. The ticket and the fine would be the punishment we would receive for breaking the law. This is the form of punishment in the works contract. The car wreck is the form of punishment in the covenant of vocation. This view of punishment is one that is not enforced from the outside, but is rather the natural consequence of our actions. So if Jesus was punished for our sins it was like the punishment of a car wreck, not a speeding ticket.

In the works contract view, somebody has to get a ticket and, fortunately for us, God the Father gave God the Son the speeding ticket that we deserved. In the covenant of vocation view, everyone is getting into car wrecks all the time. Jesus entered into our car-wrecking world and even though he wasn't speeding allowed himself to get into a car wreck in order to break the power of sin and idolatry which was the reason we have been wrecking our cars.

Consider the following diagram.

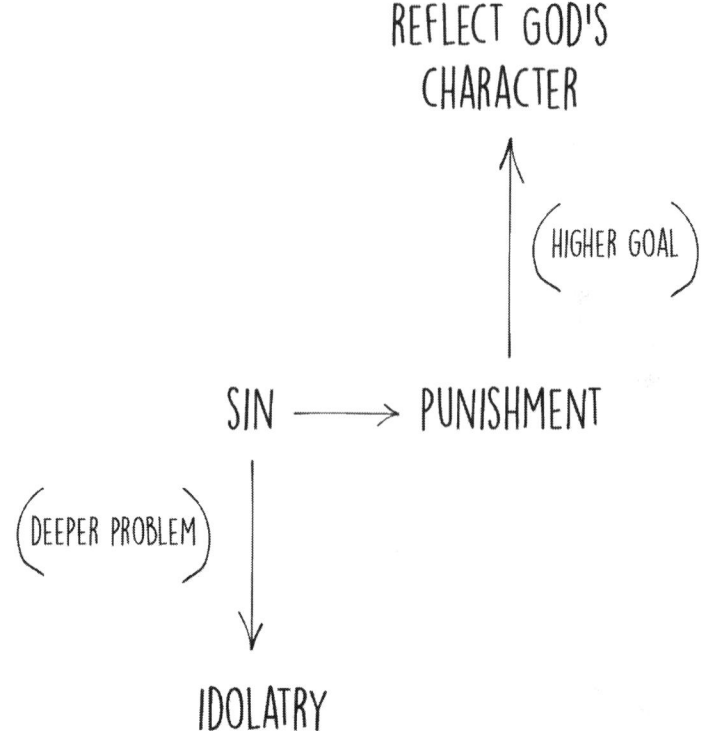

The works contract understands the problem of sin merely in terms of punishment: *God made human beings to follow the rules. The rules have been broken by sin and somebody has to be punished.* The covenant of vocation does not ignore sin and punishment, but understands that the deeper problem with sin is idolatry with all of its corrupting ways of preventing human beings from living out of their created purpose. Moreover, punishment exists not for its own sake, or for the sake of satisfying God's honor or justice. Punishment exists for a higher goal which is human beings reflecting God's character and nature into the world. From the

perspective of the covenant of vocation: *God created humanity in God's image to reflect God's love into the world. Humanity has sinned by worshipping as God that which is not God and enslaving themselves to the point where they reflect a broken image into the world. Humanity needs to be freed, healed, and transformed back into God's image-bearing creatures.* This freedom and healing comes through condemning sin and breaking the power of sin. The works contract understands punishment as *retributive*, a necessary and fair payment for sin given to humanity by God. The covenant of vocation understands punishment as *restorative*, the inherent result of sin used by God to form God's people to reflect God's image.

In Accordance with the Bible

The New Testament writers relied on the Old Testament as a foundation upon which they made known the gospel and the implications of the gospel for the church and the world. Specifically the phrases "royal priesthood" and "a kingdom of priests" draw upon the primary vocation of Israel to be the representatives of God to and for the world. The Old Testament, while made up of different kinds of writing, comprises one single sprawling story. As we read through the Old Testament we join the ancient people of God looking for the ending to their story. Israel had gone into exile in Babylon and, even though they had returned to their homeland to begin to rebuild, were still living as exiles as an occupied people. Even though they had returned to Jerusalem before the days of Jesus, their God had not.

Jesus comes as the full embodiment of Israel's God, as the ending to Israel's story. Jesus' birth, life, death, resurrection, and ascension mark the fulfillment of the law and prophets (Matthew 5:17). In Romans 10:4, Paul writes, "Christ is the end of the law." The word "end" is the Greek word *telos* which is better translated

here as "culmination." The unresolved story of Israel is a good place to start when we begin to discuss atonement and the meaning of the death of Jesus. Questions to ask ourselves as we proceed include: *What does the story of Israel with their lingering exile and the absence of the presence of God have to do with the cross of Christ? How does the death and resurrection of Jesus serve as the ending to the story of Israel?*

Reading the Old Testament and New Testament as a cohesive account of the story of redemption implies that the Jesus-conclusion makes sense only when it is read in connection with the story of Israel. The early Christians used various metaphors to describe Jesus' death and these metaphors only work together when we consider them in the context of the Old Testament.

When Paul passes on what he received of "first importance" regarding the death and resurrection of Jesus, he did so saying Jesus died for our sins "in accordance with the Scriptures" (1 Corinthians 15:3). This is not shorthand for "according to a few hand-selected Bible verses in the Old Testament," but "according to the entirety of the story told in the Old Testament." The entire story of Israel with people and a land is a direct parallel to the specific story of Adam and Eve and the garden of Eden. In this regard, the story of Israel is a picture of the larger story of all humanity and all the earth. God designed the whole world to be saturated with the life and personal presence of God. Both Israel and Adam and Eve rejected God and were sent out of the land. Adam and Eve were expelled from the garden and Israel was sent into exile, a picture of perpetual death on earth. Despite Israel's unfaithfulness, God would be faithful to the covenant, faithfulness seen ultimately in Jesus.

The problem which sent Israel into exile, the problem which Jesus becomes the answer for, is sin typified by idolatry which leads inevitably to injustice. The Greek word most often translated "sin" is the word *hamartia* meaning "missing the mark." Some Christians interpret this word as missing the mark of God's moral standard (*the*

works contract). Yet the unfolding story of Scripture describes sin as missing the mark of humanity's created purpose (*the covenant of vocation*). Humanity has failed as God's image-bearing people. When we sin we are missing the mark of our created purpose which is to reflect God's image. Since human beings become transformed by their objects of worship, sin is rooted in a failure to worship the one true living God. As we worship anything other than God (i.e. participate in idolatry) we give power to an idol to reflect an image into the world, but it is always a broken image which produces corruption in the world. We have become like spoiled children who have been invited to participate in a theater production, but instead of learning our lines and playing our part we have tossed the script to the side and done our own thing. The results are disastrous.

When empowered idols have power over God's creation, a power that God never intended them to have, they become destructive forces in the world. The dark powers unleashed by idolatry need to be overthrown so that human beings can resume their role of reflecting God's image into the world. One way to describe these powers and dark forces is "sin" or "the satan." Often we see "the satan" capitalized as "Satan," but the Hebrew word *hasatan*, best translated "the accuser," is more of a title than a personal name. Sin and the satan are connected. Sin extends beyond just an individual human problem. The widespread destruction of sin includes the unseen forces of darkness with the power to reflect a broken image into God's good world. These unseen forces keep humanity and creation itself in bondage to corruption and death. Sin from this cosmic perspective is deeply connected to idolatry, which is giving ultimate allegiance and devotion to anything other than God. "Since humans are made for the life that comes from God and God alone, to worship that which is not God is to fall in love with death" (Wright, 102).

If we think of sin as the failure to maintain God's moral standard and death as the just punishment for such failure, it is easy

to imagine Jesus' death as necessary according to divine justice so that sins may be forgiven (*the works contract*). However, this description does not sound like the big story the Scripture tells. We can handpick individual verses to force sin into that narrative, but it doesn't fit the big sweeping description of sin and redemption in the Old Testament. The failure of Israel was much more of a vocational failure than just a moral failure. The result of Israel's sin was exile, a kind of death from which they needed liberation. For exile to be undone, Israel needed both forgiveness of sin and freedom from the captors keeping them in exile. This two-fold solution implied a restoration of God's presence in and among his people.

The story of Israel's exile and hope for restoration becomes a signpost for early Christians attempting to understand the death of Jesus. A sign doesn't need to look exactly like the thing it points to. It just needs to have enough symbolism in it to point us in the right direction. Exile and restoration become very Israel-specific signs that cannot be sanitized into an abstract theory of atonement, which is why Paul speaks of the death of Jesus as a death in accordance with the Scriptures, meaning the Old Testament Scriptures. Jesus' death is the event that the sign of Israel's exile and return point us to. Traditional atonement theories may use bits of Old Testament Scripture, but they tend to ignore how the cross is connected to the very unique story unfolding in the Old Testament. To ignore the story of Israel is to pull the death of Jesus out of the Scriptures. The forgiveness of sins by the death of Jesus was necessary; Israel's sins had to be dealt with so the story of Israel could go forward, a story which has the redemption of the world as its great goal.

Within the big story the Bible tells is the story of the presence of God. In the beginning, humanity experienced the personal presence of the creator God, but very soon we see Adam and Eve hiding from God. The theme of God's presence also weaved its way through the story of Israel. God led the people of Israel through the wilderness by a cloud by day and a pillar of fire by night. God delivered them and promised to be with them. The Ark of the Covenant became a predominant item connected with the presence of God throughout Israel's wandering story. Any discussion of the mercy seat in the New Testament is in the context of this bigger story of God dwelling with his people, which is both the story of God and Israel as well as God and the world.

King David looms large in the story of Israel. God promises David a throne and a family that will endure forever. Solomon's impressive temple served only as a marker pointing to God's desire to dwell with his people ultimately through a person. The "house of David" turned out not to be a building, but a human being, the coming Messiah. Through this King, the glory of the God of Israel would fill the entire earth (Psalm 72:19). Until that time, the Temple stood as a reminder of the promise of God's glory. God's presence dwelt in the Temple until it was destroyed and the people of God were carried off into exile. The Temple had been rebuilt by the time of Jesus, but the presence of God had not returned.

John announced the return of God's glory, God's personal presence, with the coming of Jesus who is the Word made flesh who "tabernacled" among us and whose glory we beheld. John opened his gospel with these words. As we work our way through his gospel, we see the full unveiling of this glory as Jesus is hanging on the cross. The people of God of Jesus' day were not looking for rescue from an angry God threatening to send people to hell. Most Jewish people were looking for rescue within the present world. A shorthand way to communicate this rescue was by talking about "forgiveness of sins," which included a return from exile, rebuilding of the Temple, and the return of God's presence.

God's people were sent into exile because of their sins. Therefore, to be released from exile Israel's sins needed to be pardoned. Forgiveness of sins from this perspective emphasizes the heart of the revolution taking place on the cross wherein: (1) Israel's God was becoming king, (2) suffering was a necessary component, and (3) God's covenant love was being demonstrated. Israel's audacious claim to the pagan world proclaimed within their liturgy and prayers was that their God was the world's true King. The Psalms celebrate this fact particularly in Psalm 2, 46, 72, and 98. These Psalms are filled with kingdom of God language. For example, "For the LORD, the Most High, is to be feared, a great king over all the earth" (Psalm 47:2).

God had acted in the history of Israel to demonstrate his sovereign and benevolent rule. The Exodus, with its liberation from Egyptian slavery, signaled God was King indeed (Exodus 15:18). The Exodus did not include the forgiveness of sins, but the return from exile did. The expectation in the days of Jesus was for God to act in order to overthrow the pagan oppressors, bringing the exile to a full and final end. This action would be a new Exodus for the people of God, the liberation from slavery, and an act of the forgiveness of sins.

In the Old Testament and in other Jewish literature before the time of Jesus, a common theme can be found: the end of exile, which included the forgiveness of Israel's sins, was coming for the people of God, and it would come through suffering. We find no evidence in extra-biblical Jewish literature that God's coming Messiah would be the one to suffer or that Messiah would somehow die for the sins of the people. The Old Testament describes suffering during the rise of Messiah but most often it is not described as redemptive suffering (Daniel 12:1, Psalm 22:1-2, 6-7, 16-18). The only place in the Old Testament where we clearly see suffering as the means by which salvation would come to Israel is in Isaiah 53.

According to Isaiah, God's servant would be the source of salvation which would include suffering (Isaiah 53:5). In Isaiah 53 we see for the first time in the Old Testament that suffering is not only the context of the coming deliverance from exile but also the means by which that deliverance will come. Isaiah 53 includes both the language of redemptive suffering as well as victory language (Isaiah 53:12). This became a key passage for the New Testament writers describing Jesus' death. The servant of the Lord who is suffering is both Israel (Isaiah 49:3) and a person (Isaiah 52:13 ff). We begin to see how New Testament writers draw upon Isaiah 53 by reading this passage in the context of God's covenant with Israel. The suffering of God's servant would not only occur at the time of Israel's redemption; suffering would be the means by which Israel experienced the forgiveness of sins and their long awaited end of exile.

Jewish literature records the suffering of Jewish martyrs bringing an end to the suffering of God's people during the Maccabean revolt 160 years before Jesus. We find some similarities between those martyrs and the way some early Christians reflected on the death of Jesus. Some martyrs experienced punishment so that the entire nation would not experience judgment at the end. However, the description of the punishment of the Maccabean martyrs did not indicate that their deaths somehow absorbed the vengeance of God. Rather this description is similar to what Paul says in Romans 5-8 which Wright discusses later on. The concept of redemptive suffering was present in extra-biblical Jewish literature before the coming of Jesus, but not redemptive in the sense of a sacrifice to appease the wrath of God.

Isaiah 53 is important for how early Christians viewed the death of Jesus, but this chapter must be read in the larger context of God's faithful love. While the stories of the Maccabean revolt describe suffering by the Jewish martyrs, their deaths and suffering were not described in relation to God's covenant love for God's people. When looking at the Old Testament we do see a portrayal of God's anger at human rebellion and sin, but divine anger in Israel's Scriptures is not like what we see in pagan religion. Israel's God isn't an angry god that needs to be pacified. He is a loving, faithful God whose anger at human sin is portrayed as a kind of anger mixed with mourning. For Wright, "When God looks at sin, what he sees is what a violin maker would see if the player were to use his lovely creation as a tennis racquet" (Wright, 132).

We trace God's covenant love back to Deuteronomy 7:6-9 where Moses makes clear that the people of Abraham were chosen by the Lord who loved them. This theme continues through Isaiah (43:1, 3-4; 63:8-9), Jeremiah (31:3), Lamentations (3:22-23), and Hosea (11:1). In Isaiah we see that this covenant love will result in a new Exodus and this love will be extended to all the nations of the world.

Before we encounter the sufferings of the Lord's servant in Isaiah 53, we see the love and comfort coming from the Lord to his people beginning in Isaiah 40:1-52:9. The suffering servant is "wounded for our transgressions...upon him was the chastisement that brought us peace" (Isaiah 53:5) and after this time of suffering the covenant will be renewed, when the Lord will gather the people of God again (Isaiah 54:7). The picture of rescue, or salvation, we see from Deuteronomy through Isaiah is accomplished by the Lord according to his love for his people. While suffering is included in God's rescue plan, this suffering does not turn away God's anger or judgment. Rather, salvation through suffering is an expression of the Lord's love.

Three themes rise to the surface in a quick recount of the story of Israel, the ongoing exile and the unresolved story we find in the Old Testament: (1) Forgiveness of sin implied the end of exile. Israel's sin had led them into exile and God's act of forgiveness indicated that their time of enduring exile was over. (2) The expected coming salvation would be a new Exodus, where the coming Messiah would lead Israel and the world out of a slavery to sin and death. (3) Salvation and redemption would come about by the Lord himself. Isaiah's suffering servant embodies these three themes. This servant would also embody the covenant love of the Lord, bringing forth redemption for Israel and the world.

CHAPTER 2 REFLECTION QUESTIONS

1. When you were punished as a child, did you understand it as the result of:

   a) breaking the rules?
   b) disappointing your parents?
   c) your poor choices?
   d) your parents' anger?
   e) some combination of the above?

2. How have you seen people become enslaved by the idols they worship?

3. What are the key differences between God creating a system of rules for people to follow (*works contract*) and God creating a world for people to cultivate (*covenant of vocation*)?

4. What does it mean for human beings to "reflect God's image into creation"?

5. What are the differences between getting a speeding ticket and getting into a car wreck? How does this inform our understanding of how God punishes us?

6. What do we lose if we eliminate the story of Israel (the Old Testament) from our understanding of Jesus and the cross?

7. What does it mean for God's anger to be mixed with mourning, like a violin maker seeing someone use the violin like a tennis racket?

8. How does Jesus' death on the cross demonstrate the love of God?

A RENEWED COVENANT

The Day the Revolution Began, Chapters 8-9

The two disciples on the road to Emmaus who encountered the risen Jesus were waiting for (*longing for*!) the redemption of Israel. As Jesus spoke to them, he was revealing to them that indeed the redemption they were so desperately seeking had happened through his own suffering. Jesus the Messiah had come into his glorious reign as King; they just didn't know it. Israel had been redeemed through Jesus' death, but they would have to rethink what the redemption of Israel meant. God was redeeming Israel as a rescue mission to restore Israel, and thus all humanity, to their original calling to reflect God's image into the world. This reimagined hope was not about going to heaven upon death but experiencing new creation on earth. The death and resurrection of Jesus as Israel's

Messiah causes the followers of Jesus to rethink the entire story of Israel. The questions we ask at this point are two-fold: *What are human beings called to do and be in God's new creation? How is God rescuing human beings from the devastation of sin so they can become what God has called us to be?*

Wright argues that Christians have made a three-layered mistake in answering these questions: "We have Platonized our eschatology (substituting 'souls going to heaven' for the promised new creation) and have therefore moralized our anthropology (substituting a qualifying examination of moral performance for the biblical notion of the human vocation), with the result that we have paganized our soteriology, our understanding of 'salvation' (substituting the idea of 'God killing Jesus to satisfy his wrath' for the genuinely biblical notions we are about to explore)" (Wright, 147).

A Platonized eschatology describes God's future goal as discarding the physical world and taking human spirits to a non-physical heaven. The Greek philosopher Plato built a philosophical system upon the premise that the world as we experience it is not true reality, but a shadowy version of what is real. The physical universe for Plato was a hazy reflection of "the forms," pure and non-physical reality. For Wright, a Platonized eschatology is a view of the end focused entirely on souls going to heaven or hell after death. So-called "afterlife issues" find their place in a Christian understanding of end things, but when they become the sole focus, we get off course.

A moralized anthropology defines humanity's essential identity in terms of obeying God's moral laws. Anthropology is how we think of human existence, that is, the reflection upon what makes us truly human as individuals and societies. A moralized anthropology reduces our intended human purpose down to merely keeping the rules. In this view the ultimate goal for human beings is simply to please God by following the rules for no reason other than because we are supposed to. This kind of anthropology can be seen in children who are expected to follow the rules of the house not to form their character, not for any kind of higher good, but because Mom and Dad said so.

A paganized soteriology describes Jesus' death as that which necessarily satisfies the wrath of God in order for us to experience salvation. "Pagan" or "paganized" refers to concepts and practices that fall outside of the sphere of the Jewish world. In this way, a "paganized" idea is one not associated with the people of God and not necessarily one connected to ancient Roman worship or modern goddess worship. Soteriology is our thinking and talking about the nature of God's salvation. A paganized soteriology is a way of thinking about salvation that is consistent with the non-Jewish and non-Christian communities of the ancient world. The caricature very much alive in the minds of some Christians is that of a wrathful god angry at human sin demanding human sacrifice in order to satisfy God's demand for justice, thus averting God's anger. This view of God is not the picture we get from the God revealed supremely in Jesus.

Yes, we find a heavenly element in God's new creation. Yes, the human vocation contains a sense of moral obligation. Yes, the death of Jesus is both representative and substitutionary in nature. But all these themes need to be reassigned in a way consistent with the big story the Bible tells. This reassignment begins by returning to Israel's Scriptures where we find that the hope of Israel is not abandoned. Israel's hope included the forgiveness of sins, which implied not that Jewish people would go to heaven upon death, but that Israel would be redeemed and the Gentiles welcomed into the family of God.

The suffering and death of Jesus read as a fulfillment of Israel's prophecies made the forgiveness of sins possible, meaning Israel and the world were released from their captivity to sin. The goal of

God's redemption of the world through Christ was not the blessedness of heaven for those who had departed the earth in faith. This worn-out mistaken view is not what is meant by the "forgiveness of sins," a phrase which belongs to the story of Israel. Acts opens with the assumption that the kingdom had been launched. The disciples, still unaware of the significance of what has happened, asked if Jesus was going to restore the kingdom to Israel (Acts 1:6). They did not ask if they needed to go tell people their sins were forgiven so they could be assured of heaven upon death. In their minds, the work of Jesus was related to the kingdom of God on earth. Without this historical context, we can easily shrink the gospel down to a privatized faith or individual self-conditioned spirituality. Within the long winding story of Israel, the "forgiveness of sins" implied a new Passover, a new Exodus, a new covenant, and the dawning of new creation.

One of the problems with a focus on heaven instead of new creation as the goal is the modern assumption that heaven is where good people go and hell is where bad people go after they die. Some Christian traditions want to respond to this myth by saying we are all bad people, and all that has made us bad has been dealt with at the cross, and the goodness of Jesus has been added to our account, making us good. However, both this myth and the suggested response is distorted in that goodness vs. badness is placed at the center of an equation that is supposed to lead to heaven. God's new humanity has been redeemed to be a "kingdom and priests" for the world here and now.

The Kingdom of God

The restoring of the kingdom of God fulfilled three hopes for Israel: (1) freedom from Roman occupation and domination, (2) Israel's God becoming King of the world, (3) God dwelling once again with his people. We see the fulfillment of these three expectations in Acts in the theme of the kingdom of God. Modern readers tend to connect the kingdom with the second coming of Jesus, while Luke describes it as a present reality. Wright describes three kingdom symbols in Acts.

The first symbol is the restoration of worship. Jesus has ascended into heaven, joining together heaven and earth in his very person. Jesus causes us to rethink things. "In Christian theology we have to start with Jesus and reconfigure our ideas around him, rather than trying to fit him into our existing worldviews" (Wright, 162). We reject the idea of heaven as a far away spiritual place. We reject this idea in light of Jesus' ascension. When Jesus ascended into heaven, he did not merely disappear; he filled all things with himself, administering his rule through the Church of which he is the head. The followers of Jesus become the living temple, a new community where the one true living God is worshiped.

The second symbol is the witness of the Christian community to God's rule over the entire world. The principalities and powers colluded to put Jesus to death publically. As the Apostles proclaimed the gospel, the "forgiveness of sins" was communicated as a real historical event and the whole world was called upon to turn from sin and believe the good news. The rulers of this world have been defeated as God has made Jesus "both Lord and Christ" (Acts 2:36). The Apostle Paul would go on to proclaim this message throughout the Mediterranean world, enduring the suffering associated with proclaiming the kingdom of God. In God's rule, God's people are the royal priesthood doing the work of the kingdom through worship and witness.

The third symbol is the hope that Israel would be finally free from living under the rule of a pagan power, that they would truly be freed from exile. Jesus fully embodied Israel's identity becoming Israel-in-person. As Jesus was freed from death, the ultimate weapon of all pagan powers, Jesus freed Israel (and the world) from the power of foreign oppressors. In this regard, God is not rescuing people so they can escape the world; God is rescuing people so they can escape death and cooperate with God in the work of redeeming the world. This work is the work of the kingdom of God accomplished by the resurrection and ascension of Jesus and the outpouring of the Holy Spirit.

Revisiting Matthew, Mark, Luke, and John

At the very center of the book is the burning question: *How did the earliest Christians understand the death of Jesus?* The Christians during the time of the Apostles believed that something had happened with the death and resurrection of Jesus, "something as a result of which the world was now a different place. A revolution had been launched" (Wright, 169). So the pressing question as we consider the meaning of the cross is: *What changed and how did things change with the death of Jesus?* Much of the theological work on atonement has ignored the books of Matthew, Mark, Luke, and John and failed to connect the death of Jesus with the kingdom of God. The gospel writers record what Jesus said about his death and how he said it, giving us important information to help us answer our questions. The most significant bit of context regarding what Jesus said about his death is the fact that he chose the Last Supper to describe in the clearest of terms what his death meant. The Last Supper connects us to the Jewish Passover, a central and often overlooked aspect to how the early Christians understood the death of Jesus. We will return to this topic shortly, but first let's back up a moment.

If the goal of salvation is a disembodied heaven, then the gospel writers have very little to say about the implications of the death of Jesus. Furthermore, many of those who have worked on the meaning of the atonement have treated the Gospels as nothing more than the backstory to Paul's teaching on the meaning of the death of Jesus. This mistaken approach causes us to miss the contribution the Gospels make to our understanding of atonement. As we have seen, the goal of salvation is new creation and, contrary to popular approaches to the atonement, the gospel writers have much to say about the death of Jesus, each in their own way. They help us ground our exploration of the death of Jesus upon the cross in history.

The crucifixion of Jesus in its historical setting held no immediate significance other than the message of despair and defeat. No one who witnessed his death understood he was dying for the sins of the world; none of the disciples expected Messiah to die for their sins. On the day of his death, nobody was doing what we now call "atonement theology" at all. The death of Jesus was the very tragic end of a failed revolutionary and the bitter end to everyone's hopes and messianic dreams.

The catalyst for the reinterpretation of the death of Jesus was the resurrection. Many Jewish people in Jesus' day believed in the resurrection of the dead which would usher in God's new world at the end of this age. Nevertheless, followers of Jesus believed he had risen from the dead, physically and literally, *in this present age*. This central belief caused them to look back at the cross through the resurrection and, for the early Christians, this reflection did not immediately produce the atonement theories we know today. The gospel writers did not pepper their gospel accounts with atonement theories but they wove their own interpretation of the death of Jesus into the fabric of their Spirit-inspired narratives.

When we look to the four biographers of Jesus for their understanding of his death, we see first that the Roman officials who crucified Jesus displayed a sign above his head which read: "Jesus of Nazareth, King of the Jews." Jesus had regularly proclaimed the revolutionary nature of God's kingdom and therefore died as a revolutionary Jewish king. Rome regularly executed rival kings. The gospel writers not only present the death of Jesus in Roman history, but also in Jewish history. They make it clear that Jesus died around the time of the Jewish Passover. Jesus had entered into Jerusalem with shouts of "Hosanna!" Jesus challenged Jerusalem one last time while the nation was celebrating God's act of freeing them from slavery in Egypt. Jesus chose Passover for this final proclamation of God's coming kingdom because the breaking in of God's kingdom implied the overthrow of enslaving powers. Moses confronted Pharaoh before the Exodus; Jesus confronted the Temple establishment before his death. Israel was leaving Egypt in order to worship God; Jesus' death and soon-to-follow resurrection would reimagine worship and the meaning of the Temple for the renewed people of God. Jesus' death was a new Exodus.

Jesus describes the meaning of his own death in the clearest of terms as he is with his disciples in the Upper Room sharing a Passover meal with them. According to Wright, "When Jesus wanted to explain to his followers what his forthcoming death was all about, he did not give them a theory, a model, a metaphor, or any other such thing; he gave them a meal" (Wright, 182). Jesus transformed the Passover meal from looking back towards the Exodus to looking forward to his pending death. The cup of wine was the "blood of the covenant which is poured out for many for the forgiveness of sins" (Matthew 26:28). The death of Jesus would be an experience of liberation and victory and the launch of God's kingdom. Jesus connected his death with the Passover tradition.

Victory over the powers of slavery was secured as Jesus' death dealt with the sins of Israel and the sins of the world. The Jewish people were still experiencing exile. Even though they were in their ancestral homeland, they were still in bondage to the powers of their Roman oppressors. This new Exodus event coming through the death of Jesus would be an act of forgiveness of sins and thus the long-awaited end to exile. With the Last Supper in sight, we can rescue our discussions about the cross from the pagan ideas of a wrathful god demanding satisfaction. When reflecting back on the God of the Passover, we see in Jesus a covenant-faithful God taking sin upon himself in order to move the story of redemption forward. Atonement from the perspective of this sacred meal is more of a story for Christians to enter than an abstract theory to try to understand. Sharing in the bread and the cup makes followers of Jesus active participants in God's story.

Jesus makes mention of the "blood of the covenant" as he lifts the cup in the Passover meal pointing to the sacrificial overtones of his death. Drinking blood would have been unimaginable for Jesus' Torah-observant followers. In the face of scandal and controversy, Jesus connects the cup with blood, covenant, and the forgiveness of sins, pointing to Jeremiah's prophecy of a new covenant which is itself rooted in the Exodus event (Jeremiah 31:31-34). Jesus connected the shedding of his blood to the blood of animals, which were not being punished when they were sacrificed. We have seen that early Christians understood Jesus died "according to the Scripture," that is, in accordance with the story the Bible is telling. This story included the suffering not only by God's people but the future suffering of God's servant who would do for Israel what Israel could not do for herself. In embodying the identity of Israel, God's servant would also remain faithful to the covenant and vocation of Israel to be a light to the Gentile world.

Jesus as the servant of the Lord offered forgiveness throughout his ministry as he was announcing the arrival of the kingdom of God. As we have seen, the announcement of the forgiveness of sins implied the end of exile, the liberation from oppressive powers, and a renewal of the covenant. Jesus offered forgiveness with great compassion and mercy, explaining to his disciples "the Son of Man came not to be served but to serve, and to give his life as a ransom for many"

(Matthew 20:28). Jesus wasn't offering his disciples an abstract theological principle to understand his sacrificial death; he was summing up his entire life mission. Jesus was giving his life as a ransom because of his great love which remained "to the end" (John 13:1).

The offering of his life, as Jesus announced at the Last Supper, was an announcement of the coming of the kingdom from heaven to earth. Jesus renewed the covenant as Israel's representative substitute, taking upon himself the vocation and fate of Israel, laying down his life for his friends (John 15:13). Theories of the atonement grow out of the story of Jesus as Jesus' entire life and ministry guide us in understanding the meaning of his death. Without the foundational story of Jesus found in the Gospels, a story rooted in the story of Israel, the death of Jesus too easily becomes a "paganized doctrine" where an innocent person dies to appease an angry deity. With these stories in view, Paul's summaries of what happened when Jesus died become much clearer, namely that God, the God of Israel, the Creator God, was in Christ "reconciling the world to himself" (2 Corinthians 5:19). Through Jesus' death the covenant to bless the nations of the earth through the people of Abraham was renewed. For Wright, "The cross became the encoded symbol as well as the actual outworking of the dying, and hence the undying, love of Israel's God" (Wright, 194).

CHAPTER 3 REFLECTION QUESTIONS

1. When you first heard of salvation, "getting saved," or "accepting Christ" was it in the context of the assurance of heaven after you died? What were your earliest memories of salvation?

2. If God is an angry deity demanding blood to satisfy his wrath, what would that communicate to us about the nature of God?

3. Why do you think it is still a cultural assumption that "good guys go to heaven and bad guys go to hell"?

4. Why is it important to start with Jesus and reconfigure our ideas around him when we are trying to understand the nature and work of God?

5. Look again at Matthew 26:28. What does Jesus say about his death here?

6. Look again at Jeremiah 31:31-34. What does this say about the new covenant that was fulfilled in and through Jesus?

7. Why is it necessary to understand the story of Israel in order to understand why Jesus died?

8. How would you describe the love of God you see revealed in Jesus' life, ministry, and death?

THE KINGDOM TRIUMPH OVER THE POWERS

The Day the Revolution Began, Chapters 10-11

When Jesus talks about the kingdom of heaven as recorded in Matthew's gospel, he is not talking about a place called "heaven" where we go upon death, but the "rule of heaven," the kingdom of God. The warnings Jesus gives associated with hell are often directed toward pending disaster in this world, namely the imminent destruction of Jerusalem in 70 AD, even if some references to hell, (Greek word *gehenna)*, seem to point to something beyond calamity in this world. (For example see Matthew 10:28 and Luke 12:4-5.) If the gospel writers could talk to modern American evangelicals, they would most certainly confirm they were proclaiming the gospel in the narratives they were constructing. Modern evangelical speculative theories, and propensity to hand-pick individual verses of Scripture, have turned the atonement into a mechanism rather than the crucial moment when God's revolutionary kingdom was launched.

While the gospel writers have tended to be ignored when we turn to the Scripture to understand the meaning of the cross, the time has come to turn up the volume on Matthew, Mark, Luke, and John in order to hear their stories loud and clear—stories about the kingdom, the Temple, Pilate, and the mocking crowd. By giving them our attention we can hear the big story they are telling. Listening to these stories guides our journey towards understanding what exactly happened the day Jesus died. During this quest we will find both historical answers and theological answers.

Historically, Jesus died because the chief priests saw Jesus' ministry as blasphemous. The Romans saw Jesus as a rival king. The Pharisees held Jesus in contempt for challenging their rules. The followers of Jesus abandoned him, including one who betrayed him. Our search for theological answers, for the divine reason Jesus died, cannot continue without taking into consideration the historical answers. For Wright, "The historical questions and answers are the place to go if we want to find the theological answer" (Wright, 199). Our purpose in paying attention to the historical questions in the Gospels is to determine Jesus' own understanding of his mission and purpose.

When we listen to the gospel writers we can hear them telling the story of Jesus as the long-awaited return of Israel's God. In fact, they intentionally connect the Jesus story with the story of Israel. Jesus came as the Son of God, the living embodiment of Israel's God, and Emmanuel, God with us. The Gospel writers portray the life and ministry of Jesus as one filled with compassion and love.

Jesus' death is the tragic end of the one who embodied the covenant-keeping love of Israel's God. The Spirit-led writers, particularly John, described the growing hostility towards Jesus ending in his public execution (see John 5:18, 7:1, 7:19-20, 7:25, 8:37-40). Jesus came to his own, representing all humanity, and they wanted him dead.

The Battle with Evil

Within the story the gospel writers are telling is not only the story of Israel but the story of darkness and evil that has plagued God's good world since the beginning of human civilization. Evil has been depicted throughout the story of Israel in various forms of idolatry and injustice not only by pagans but by members of the people of God. The patriarchs and the kings, the heroes in the up-and-down story of Israel were all flawed, hindered by the presence of evil and sin. Evil is not merely a pagan problem but a disease affecting all people and all of creation.

The storm clouds were forming around Jesus from his birth as Herod sought to kill him before his ministry even got started. The poor responded to his ministry, but his kingdom message did not draw applause from the ruling Jewish elite. The Pharisees opposed him. The chief priests sought to kill him. Rome saw him as a political threat. He taught the way of peace, reconciliation, and self-sacrifice, which eclipsed all the traditional Jewish cultural markers. All of this animosity and opposition revealed how evil coalesced into a single force putting Jesus to death. Jesus had not been battling people and their evil ideas as much as he had been fighting evil itself. As Jesus drew near to his death, he told his disciples, "Now is the judgment of this world; now will the ruler of this world be cast out. And I, when I am lifted up from the earth, will draw all people to myself" (John 12:31-32). Jesus' death would be a victory over evil by casting out the unseen evil ruling forces behind the visible evil structures in the world. This victory was not placed artificially over the story of Israel but reached its climax within the story itself.

In this way we can read the Gospels as both the coming of God's kingdom being the culmination of Israel's story and the story of how evil came together against Jesus who then took upon himself the weight of sin, and subsequently defeated death, evil, and sin. In Acts 4, as the followers of Jesus were praying, they quoted from Psalm 2 acknowledging that "the rulers were gathered together, against the Lord and against his Anointed" (Acts 4:26). Evil had gathered together in Herod and Pilate at the trial of Jesus, just as Psalm 2 said. When Jesus was arrested he told the chief priests and the temple guards, "this is your hour, and (the hour of the) power of darkness" (Luke 22:53). Jesus was not in a battle against flesh and blood but against the power of darkness itself.

This power of darkness is the satan, the "ruler of this world," who will be cast out by Jesus' death. The satan entered Judas turning him into "the accuser." This battle with evil isn't a convenient backdrop to the death of Jesus which is about something altogether different. Particularly in John's gospel, the meaning of the death of Jesus is connected to the story John tells, a story of struggle and death, victory and love, a story of Jesus' death as the defeat of evil according to God's covenant love. As we have seen, the Gospel writers convey to us the words of Jesus about his death at the Passover. Jesus is the Passover lamb who, in the words of John the Baptist, "takes away the sin of the world" (John 1:29). As sin is taken away, a great victory over the power of evil has been won. The coming Messiah rules in the proclamation of God's kingdom by putting an end to sin. The great themes of God's kingdom rule and the redemption of the world through the cross are inextricably tied together in the Gospels.

Forgiveness of sins and thus the end of exile comes about because Jesus bears the punishment of Israel. Jesus also brings an end to exile by redefining the shape of the kingdom of God by his very death. The kingdom of God, in contrast to first century Jewish expectations, looks like self-giving love and self-denial. As Israel's representative, Jesus does what Israel was called to do but ultimately couldn't do, namely their calling to represent the light of God's truth to the Gentile world. Jesus said, "As Moses lifted up the serpent in the wilderness, so must the Son of man be lifted up," a symbolic reference to his death (John 3:14). As Jesus was lifted up on the cross, the sin and death that had plagued not only Israel but all mankind were brought together. When we see the cross and gaze upon the suffering of Jesus we realize our sins have been dealt with. According to Jesus, his death was not to appease an angry God, but rather to demonstrate the love of God, "For God so loved the world, that he gave his only Son...." (John 3:16).

Jesus died as a rebel in the place of rebellious Israel, as depicted in the crowd's desire for Barabbas to be released and Jesus to be crucified. The gospel writers make it clear that Jesus was innocent. He had done nothing wrong yet was sentenced to death. Even as he hung on the cross, the penitent thief being crucified with Jesus announced that Jesus had done no wrong (Luke 23:41). Jesus promised "paradise," a restful holdover until resurrection, to this thief. Within Luke's gospel we see the powers of darkness defeated because Jesus dies on behalf of the guilty. Throughout his ministry, Jesus had warned people of coming disaster—not going to hell after death, but real world disaster. Hell in the afterlife is a reality not to be overlooked, but it is not the primary form of disaster Jesus was talking about.

Jesus died as a substitute in that Jesus represents Israel as their Messiah. Jesus bore the weight of Israel's sins and the sins of the world and died as the forces of evil colluded against him so at long last the kingdom of God could come. The death of Jesus is what it looks like when Israel's God becomes king of the nations, but it does not look like conventional power. This surprising death of King Jesus revealed that the power of the kingdom of God is the power of co-suffering, self-giving love. The kingdom is therefore launched not by the elites of society but by the poor, the meek, the mourning, and the peacemakers. The kingdom will not come through the military might of empire, but through the way of nonviolence, enemy-love, and prayers for persecutors.

By his death Jesus set forth a new way of life, the way of love and reconciliation that will become the way by which God redeems the world. The death of Jesus does not save us *from* the world by taking us to heaven; rather, the death of Jesus saves us *for* the world, a powerful revolution within the world, a vision found among Israel's prophets. Israel was always called to be the means by which the kingdom of God would come, but the means by which the revolution began took most of Israel by surprise. The Messiah came into this world born of a virgin in Bethlehem, with the words of peace and forgiveness on his lips. The very nature of power had to be radically reimagined by the followers of King Jesus. According to Wright, "A new sort of power will be let loose upon the world, and it will be the power of self-giving love. This is the heart of the revolution that was launched on Good Friday" (Wright, 222). The powers are overthrown by the death of Jesus in part because Jesus was powerless in his death.

As we step back for a bird's-eye view of what we see in the death of Jesus in the Gospels, we find the following predominant landmarks. First, the gospel writers do not give us bits of information that we need to factor into a formula or theory about what the death of Jesus really means; rather, the meaning of Jesus' death is found in what they have written. According to Wright, the "formula" is in fact a "portable narrative, a folded-up story" (Wright, 223). We must resist any attempt to understand the death of Jesus apart from the historical context, which has much to say about the kingdom of God coming to earth.

Second, before we begin to look at how Paul deals with the cross in his letters, we acknowledge the revolutionary and kingdom nature of the cross. In this wide-angle view of the cross, we do not lose the truth that Jesus died for our sins, which has personal implications for all those who believe. Individual faith and responsibility are still intact, but as modern individuals we are invited into a larger story that is more than going to heaven when we die. We find ourselves in a story of creation, covenant, and new creation, a story we repeat as we come to the communion table, a story we live out as we cooperate with the Spirit's work of peacemaking and reconciliation.

From The Gospels to Paul

The Apostle Paul had much to say about the death of Jesus. Traditional atonement theories have had the tendency to look first to Paul, running right past the Gospels and much of the Old Testament. But just as we want to ground our understanding of the death of Jesus in its historical context, we also want to ground our reading of Paul in his historical context. Paul used a variety of different images to describe the cross of Christ. We can develop a singular vision of atonement based on only one of these images, which some have done with the penal substitution theory from the perspective of the works contract. We do find both "penal" (that is having to do with punishment) and "substitutionary" (that is having to do with someone standing in the place of another) aspects to the death of Jesus. However a fresh reading of the New Testament reveals that these expression of atonement occur within the story of the new Exodus in Christ and not within the story of a wrathful God in need of satisfaction.

There are two overarching concepts to keep in mind as we look at Paul's understanding of the cross: (1) the story of redemption is moving towards new creation and (2) the death of Jesus is the means by which new creation is attained. With new creation in its proper place as the goal instead of "going to heaven," we avoid the mistaken Platonized eschatology. Jesus takes upon himself the divine condemnation of sin on behalf of Israel and the world. This sacrificial act becomes the supreme revelation of God's love, the very covenant-faithful love we see throughout the story of Israel. Paul unapologetically proclaims the power of the cross without explaining precisely why or how the cross has the power it has (1 Corinthians 1:18). So while we don't know how the cross is powerful, we do know the effects of the cross which include both the salvation of those who believe and the driving out of the "rulers of this age" (1 Corinthians 2:6).

As we have discovered, Paul delivered to his churches what he received that "Christ died for our sins in accordance with the Scriptures" (1 Corinthians 15:3). In other words, Jesus the Messiah died for our sins according to the story of Israel. The expectation of Jewish believers in Jesus was that the death (and ultimate resurrection) of Jesus would establish the kingdom of God (see Luke 23:42, Acts 1:6). The various images Paul used are not random metaphors but all find their cohesion and definition in the Old Testament. Behind all Paul revealed about the death of Jesus stands this central truth: Jesus died as Israel's Messiah. The English word "Christ" comes from the Greek word *christos* which means "anointed one." The Jewish tradition was not to crown their kings, but to anoint them with oil. The Hebrew word for "anointed one" is *mashiach*, best transliterated in English as "Messiah." Christ, or Messiah, was the Jewish title for their king.

The metaphors Paul used to describe both the death of Jesus and its effects including sacrifice, atonement, redemption, deliverance, justification, victory, and rescue all bring resolution to the previously unresolved story of Israel. When we make the death of Jesus only about individual sinners going to heaven when they die, we lose the story of Israel, the very context we need to make sense of what Paul wrote. The goal of new creation underscores God's promises to Abraham to be the father of many nations, where Gentiles would come and worship the God of Israel (Romans 15:8-9). Let's take a brief look at what Paul said about the death of Jesus in various letters. We will look at Paul's letter to the Romans in the next chapter.

Within Paul's letter to the Galatians we never find the words "saved" or "salvation," emphasizing the fact that this letter is not about individuals "getting saved." Rather the letter is about unity, that is, the fulfillment of God's promises to Abraham of a single family made up of Jews and Gentiles worshipping the God of Israel as a unified family. Paul spoke of Jesus "who gave himself for our sins to deliver us from the present evil age" (Galatians 1:4). Deliverance is Passover language, pointing the death of Jesus towards a new Passover. The "present evil age" and the "age to come" are standard ways of talking about Jewish eschatology. We are delivered from this present age dominated by sin and evil and hurled forward into the age to come dominated by love and peace.

Paul summed up his unity letter to the Galatians by pointing to what really matters—new creation (Galatians 6:15), a very present reality because through the resurrection of Jesus the new age has broken into the present evil age. Jesus' death has abolished the power of the old world. In this new creation world, Gentiles are now welcomed into the family of Abraham. The law of Moses was a temporary guardian (Galatians 3:24), but now Jesus has come and redeemed us.

Redemption is Exodus language. We were slaves to sin like Israel was enslaved in Egypt; Jesus came to rescue not only Israel but the whole world through his death and resurrection. Now Jews and Gentiles have full knowledge of God through Jesus and the Spirit. The need for circumcision has passed away with the old world. Jesus has redeemed Israel from the curse of the law (Galatians 3:13), a reference to Deuteronomy. The blessings and curses in Deuteronomy were not bestowed on individuals but on Israel as a whole. Paul does not say Jesus bore the curse so that individual Gentiles could be forgiven. This new Exodus for Israel would require new thinking about what identified people as members of God's family. Jesus bore the curse so that the promises made to Abraham could be fulfilled, that the blessing to Abraham would be extended to the Gentiles.

Galatians 3:10-14 is "penal" and "substitutionary" but not according to the traditional narrative coming out of the Reformation. This section of Galatians is best read within the context of the covenant of vocation. Exile is over because the curse has fallen on Jesus as Israel's substitute or representative, thus freeing Israel so she could be liberated to fulfill her vocation as a light to the Gentiles. As Israel's representative Jesus can act as a substitute. Jesus enters into the story of Israel and receives Israel's curse so the story of redemption for the world can move forward. The problem with Israel is not her sin in general, but that her sin has stalled the promise of worldwide redemption. When sins are forgiven, the powers are robbed of power so that the goal of new creation, including the promises made to Abraham, can be reached.

Along with this new Passover/new Exodus journey toward new creation, we also have a new identity. Each person in Christ can now say, "I have been crucified with Christ. It is no longer I who live, but Christ who lives in me. And the life I now live in the flesh I live by faith in the Son of God, who loved me and gave himself for me" (Galatians 2:20). While most of Paul's descriptions of salvation were plural, he did speak of himself in the singular as having a reshaped identity in Christ. Paul lived "within the faithfulness of the Son of God," a better translation than "faith in the Son of God." The revolutionary nature of the cross changes how we look at ourselves. We identify ourselves by the cross; if we were to identify ourselves by the Jewish law there would be no reason for Jesus to die (Galatians 2:21).

Wright offers three points regarding the connection of the death of Jesus and the inclusion of Gentiles into the family of God in Galatians. First, God has condemned the present evil age and inaugurated the "age to come," freeing all people from evil and sin. Second, God has done this through the death of Jesus who died for our sins. In Christ no one is labeled "unclean" or "excluded from the family of God." Third, Jews in Christ have a radical new identity formed around the death and resurrection of Jesus.

Galatians is about unity in Christ, although older interpretations of Galatians going back to the Reformation tend to read it as a text advising the Church not to attempt to earn "righteousness" or salvation by good works. Any attempt to read a rebuke of "legalism" in Galatians is to miss Paul's point. The old age is passing away, including the works of the flesh (Galatians 5:19-21) associated with that age. The Spirit-driven age to come ushers in a new lifestyle typified by the fruit of the Spirit (Galatians 5:22-23). Moral energy and emotional effort for those in Christ are not connected to earning one's salvation, but to recognizing what has happened in Christ. The yoke of sin has been broken in Christ and we are now free to pursue God with all we are. This new Passover event was the means towards the kingdom's triumph over the powers of the present evil age holding us captive. A new kind of unity and holiness for the people of God is the appropriate response to this revolution. To live according to the ethics of the present evil age is to deny that the age to come has arrived through the death and resurrection of Jesus.

As with the book of Galatians, Paul does not give us a clear explanation in 1 Corinthians concerning how or why the death of Jesus accomplished what it does, but Paul does continue to use Passover imagery, "For Christ, our Passover lamb, has been sacrificed" (1 Corinthians 5:6). Jesus connected the practice of communion with the "new covenant in my blood." For Christians, the practice of communion became the "proclamation of the Lord's death" (1 Corinthians 11:25-26). We have seen Paul's important statement regarding the death of Christ "for our sins in accordance with the Scriptures" (1 Corinthians 15:3). This sacrificial death and the resurrection that follows defeated sin and death for us that we may share in his victory (1 Corinthians 15:57). Jesus' inauguration of the kingdom of God through death overturned all conventional approaches to power.

The followers of Jesus exercise power on the earth through suffering: "For we who live are always being given over to death for Jesus' sake, so that the life of Jesus also may be manifested in our mortal flesh" (2 Corinthians 4:11). The cross is not simply a mechanism by which salvation occurs. The cross shapes our lives as followers of Jesus and the cross reveals to us what God is like. According to Wright, "The Messiah's crucifixion unveiled the very nature of God himself at work in generous self-giving love to overthrow all power structures by dealing with the sin that had given them their power, that same divine nature would now be at work through the ministry of the gospel not only through what was said, but through the character and the circumstances of the people who were saying it" (Wright, 251). This understanding of the cross fits within the covenant of vocation. The cross was the means by which our sins are dealt with and the cross becomes the way we live as the image-bearing creatures of the Creator God.

According to Paul, in Christ we have entered into God's new creation and have received a job, the ministry of reconciliation (2

Corinthians 5:17-18). God in Christ was reconciling the world to himself, not so we could keep the rules according to the works contract, but so we could be agents of reconciliation in God's world: "For our sake he made him to be sin who knew no sin, so that in him we might (embody) the righteousness of God" (2 Corinthians 5:21).

Those working from the perspective of the works contract see in this verse what has been called "double imputation," where our sin was imputed to Christ and his "righteousness" was imputed to us. However, in the context of the ministry of reconciliation (and the larger context of the covenant of vocation), Paul was not talking about a righteousness *we receive* but a righteousness *we embody*. The "righteousness of God" in this verse is not a moralistic status but a covenant status. God's own righteousness, or "rightness," speaks of God's fidelity to the covenant. God made him, Jesus, who knew no sin to bear our sins, taking them away through his death, so we could embody God's faithfulness to the covenant. Jesus, in reflection of God's love, dies innocently on behalf of the guilty that we might be restored in order to reflect God's fidelity and love into all creation.

In Philippians Paul recorded what was either an ancient hymn or poem (see Philippians 2:6-11). At the very heart of this poem is the line "even death on the cross." This poem tells the story of Jesus with the cross at the center. In the great crescendo, we see the victory of Jesus over all powers and creatures in heaven, on earth, and under the earth. This exaltation of Jesus is kingdom language marking the inauguration of the kingdom of God led by King Jesus. The poem also noted that Jesus took the "form of a servant," echoing Isaiah 40-55 and the servant of the Lord. The kingdom of God is established precisely by destroying the power of idolatry and taking away the power of sin and death.

According to Colossians 2:13-15, Jesus at the cross disarmed "the rulers and authorities." These ruling powers are both the earthly rulers of Rome and their appointees (namely King Herod in the Judean province of the Roman Empire), as well as the invisible rulers, the dark forces that manipulate earthly power structures. Jesus in his death triumphs over them, putting them to shame, because their system of power and domination results in putting to death not just an innocent man but God in human flesh.

Earthly rulers are able to rule through the power of punishment (i.e. death) and through the enslaving power of idolatry. In ancient Rome the Caesar was worshipped as divine and the pantheon of gods offered idolatry to the masses. When human beings worship in the place of God that which is not God, corruption of their humanity begins. But through the death of Jesus sins are forgiven and taken away, breaking the power of sin and idolatry and reconciling broken humanity to their Creator. In this act the invisible powers at work within idolatry lose their power.

CHAPTER 4 REFLECTION QUESTIONS

1. Why is the story of Israel in the Old Testament important to understanding the story of Jesus in the New Testament?

2. Where in the Gospels do you see Jesus confronting different kinds of expressions of evil?

3. What are the key differences between how the kingdoms of this world exercise power and how power is exercised in the God's kingdom?

4. How have you found a new identity in Christ who died for your sins and gave himself up for you?

5. Describe in your own words what it means for the age to come to have broken into the present evil age.

6. What are some of the challenges of living as people of the age to come in the present evil age as related to global issues like terrorism, war, poverty, and racism?

7. What does the cross reveal about the nature of God?

8. What is the difference between becoming the righteousness of God and embodying the righteousness of God?

THE DEATH OF JESUS IN ROMANS

*The Day the Revolution Began,
Chapters 12-13*

Romans is a wonderfully challenging and complex letter. In reading it we are at times standing on our feet applauding the poetic brilliance of Paul and at other times we are sitting, scratching our heads trying to make sense of where Paul is going with certain themes. Nevertheless, in various places Paul states explicitly what the first Christians believed about the cross such as "God shows his love for us in that while we were still sinners, Christ died for us" (Romans 5:8, see also Romans 3:25-26, 4:24-25, 7:4, 8:3-4). Too often the first four chapters of Romans have been read from the mistaken perspective of the works contract. Worse yet, the entire letter has been wrongly summed up in the popular "Romans Road" which skips through Romans missing Paul's underlying points.

There are three important things to keep in mind as we begin to see how Paul describes the death of Jesus and its effects in this book of the Bible. First, Romans is a tightly woven, orderly, sophisticated letter with four identifiable sections connected together in a subtle but cohesive way. Second, Romans is not a collection of theological doctrines for us to pull out and examine in isolation. People have often gone to Romans looking to understand the doctrine of justification, missing both the context and the other important themes in the letter. Third, the letter underscores the goal of salvation as not going to heaven but new creation and the restoration of God's image-bearing creatures to their intended role in God's good creation.

According to Romans 1:18, the problem with humanity is not just sin, but ungodliness (Greek word *asebeia*), best translated as a "lack of proper respect for God." In other words, human beings do not simply have a problem with behavior but with worship. We have routinely worshipped the creation rather than the Creator. This expression of idolatry has led us into sinful behavior (Romans 1:22-23). Paul uses homosexual activity as an example of the root problem of ungodliness (Romans 1:26) not because sexual acts between people of the same gender are themselves the root problem. Sexual immorality in all of its forms occurs when we worship sexual love over the God and creator of love. "Sin" is how Paul regularly describes the brokenness of humanity, but it's more than just acts of willful disobedience. Free from sin, humanity in Christ is now enabled to share in Jesus' ministry "in the priestly service of the gospel of God" (Romans 15:16). So how has the death of Jesus responded to this problem of sin, ungodliness, and idolatry?

We can quickly go to Romans 3:21-26 for answers, but this passage is a part of a different argument Paul is making about God's righteousness, or covenant faithfulness. We will return to Romans 3:21-26 in a moment, but first let's walk through the rest of Romans to get an overview. Some have argued Romans 1-4 describes sin and what God did about it, while Romans 5-8 is about other associated topics. Romans 5-8 is the second section of the four sections of Romans, and in these chapters we find more references to the death of Jesus than in any other section in Romans. Paul's recurring theme in Chapters 5-8 and throughout Romans is the new Exodus, the freedom from slavery to sin, and the journey to renewed creation.

Romans 5:1-5 sums up Romans 3:21-4:25, the long passage about justification by faith, a subject we will return to momentarily. The experience of justification produces a hope rooted in God's love poured into our hearts by the Holy Spirit (Romans 5:5), a love Paul celebrates in Romans 8:31-39 at the climax of the letter. While Paul does not explicitly explain how, he writes "we were reconciled to God by the death of his Son" (Romans 5:10). This reconciliation for those "justified by his blood" includes being "saved by him from the wrath of God" (Romans 5:9). "Wrath" is that which is revealed from heaven against ungodliness (Romans 1:18) and is being stored up by those with stubborn unrepentant hearts (Romans 2:5). Wrath here speaks of God's eschatological judgment. Most English translations of Romans 5:9 include the words "of God," but the Greek text only says "the wrath." Paul here uses "the wrath" as a metaphor. God doesn't have literal anger any more than God has literal eyes or arms.

With hope secured in Christ, "those who receive the abundance of grace" will "reign in life through the one man Jesus Christ" (Romans 5:17). This "reign in life" refers to sharing in the reign of God, the kingdom of God. Through the death of Christ the covenant of vocation is back on track. The free gift of righteousness whereby "many will be made righteous" (Romans 5:19) speaks not of our moral standing before God; it speaks of our standing within God's covenant family. The gift of righteousness for Wright is the "gift of covenant membership" where we are declared "in the right" and thus members of the one people of God. The Mosaic law increased sin which produced the kingdom of death. Grace as a summation of the work of Jesus through his life, death, and resurrection produces the kingdom of God's covenant faithfulness and justice.

Romans 6-8 with its description of the struggle with sin in Romans 7 and the new life in the Spirit in Romans 8 is not a picture of the "normal Christian life," one of ongoing cycles of struggle and triumph. Rather these chapters fully expand what Paul wrote in Romans 3:24-26 about the redemption found in Christ Jesus. "Redemption" is a word drawn from the Exodus. These chapters form a picture of the new Exodus in Jesus.

Romans 6:2-11 depicts baptism as the means by which we identify with the death of Jesus in order that we may "walk in newness of life" (Romans 6:4). Sin becomes personified as the slavemaster, and baptism becomes a picture of the crossing of the Red Sea where the people of God leave behind the slavery of Egypt for a new life in God's Promised Land. Jesus has died and through his resurrection "death no longer has dominion over him" (Romans 6:9). We were enslaved to sin (Romans 6:16) but Jesus has died to sin, freeing us from the dominion of sin and death. With these words Paul draws upon the Passover theme as well as the theme of the end of exile through the forgiveness of sins.

In Romans 7:4, Paul reemphasized this point. We have died to the law through Jesus' death "in order that we may bear fruit for God," a reference back to Jesus' words in John 15:5 and the words of Isaiah in Isaiah 32:16, 45:8. Our covenant of vocation to be image-bearers of God is the fruit God is looking for. What Paul described is a new Exodus movement, a kingdom of God movement, that works because Jesus represents his people; what happened to him happened to us. He died and was raised. In Christ we die to sin and are raised to newness of life. Jesus is both our representative and our substitute. Sin with its enslaving power has been defeated. None of this can be reduced to simple formulas or quick and easy summaries outside of "Christ died for our sins in accordance with the Scriptures."

The death of Jesus finds its deepest meaning in the story of Israel. For Wright, "Every step away from the Jewish narrative, in this case the Jewish narrative as reaching its focal point in Israel's Messiah, is a step towards paganism" (Wright, 281). Within the works contract view, Israel is just an example of people not keeping God's rules, and Abraham is nothing more than an example of how individuals develop a relationship with God by being justified by faith. From the perspective of the covenant of vocation, Israel is the very means by which God remains faithful to Abraham to rescue and bless all the families of the earth.

Much of what Paul is wrestling with in Romans is the role of the Jewish Law. In Romans 7:7-8:3, Paul makes the argument that the law pulled together sin into a single point so that sin could be condemned once and for all. The struggle with sin, described in Romans 7, is described by Paul in the first person ("I do not do what I want, but I do the very thing I hate." —Romans 7:15). This use of the first person is a "rhetorical I." Paul is speaking of himself as a representative of all of Israel under the law.

Rather than telling a personal story about one man's struggle with sin, Romans 7 tells the story of Israel which is on a large scale the story of Adam and Eve—sin personified as a force of evil, "seizing an opportunity through the commandment deceived me and through it killed me," according to Paul (Romans 7:11). Sin killed Israel through the giving of the law, which is itself good and holy. God gave the law not for sin to have its opportunity, but so God could do what God did next. Through the law and in Israel sin was gathered together into a single point so God could condemn it in the flesh of Jesus who is Israel-in-person.

If we see any kind of "penal" aspect in Paul's letter, it is in Romans 8:3: "For God has done what the law, weakened by the flesh, could not do. By sending his own Son in the likeness of sinful flesh and for sin, he condemned sin in the flesh." God did not punish Jesus. Rather, God punished sin in the flesh of Jesus. God declares that those in Christ are in the right, in the covenant family (Romans 5:19), and God declares sin condemned. In this way Jesus' death is substitutionary. Sin has been condemned and now there is no condemnation for those in Christ.

Sin has now finally been dealt with, rescuing people from its enslaving power in the cross which is the new Passover event, the new Exodus, leading people into new creation. Within the story of ancient Israel and in Jesus as the conclusion of that story, we find the meaning of the death of Jesus. In sending the Son, God was sending himself. God initiated a covenant with Abraham and remained faithful to the covenant in and through Jesus. Those who have been justified in Jesus are now justice-bringers with Jesus living as expressions of God's love. Wright asks, "What if the Creator, all along, had made the world out of overflowing, generous love, so that the overflowing, self-sacrificial love of the Son going to the cross was indeed the accurate and precise self-expression of the love of God for a world radically out of joint?" (Wright, 293).

The Key Passage in Romans

We now turn our attention back to Romans 3:21-26, this very important, very densely packed, and very hotly debated passage in

Paul's letter to the Romans. Wright quotes this passage from the NRSV, which he calls "the least problematic" translation (Wright, 295). I am working with the ESV which has some issues that we will address below. Here is the text in its entirety:

"But now the righteousness of God has been manifested apart from the law, although the Law and the Prophets bear witness to it—the righteousness of God through faith in Jesus Christ for all who believe. For there is no distinction: for all have sinned and fall short of the glory of God, and are justified by his grace as a gift, through the redemption that is in Christ Jesus, whom God put forward as a propitiation by his blood, to be received by faith. This was to show God's righteousness, because in his divine forbearance he had passed over former sins. It was to show his righteousness at the present time, so that he might be just and the justifier of the one who has faith in Jesus" (Romans 3:21-26).

There are two things to keep in mind before diving into this text. First, as we have seen, early Christians saw Jesus' death as connected to Passover, the Exodus event, and thus the great "forgiveness of sins" event. Second, Romans 1-4 should be read as a whole with Romans 3:21-26 as the center of the argument Paul is making. If we remove this text from its connection to the Jewish Passover and the entire context of Paul's thought process in Romans 1-4, we will misunderstand Paul's point. We will end up defaulting to the works contract and wrongly assume Paul in Romans 3:21-26 is describing how: (1) humans in general sin, breaking God's rules, (2) Jesus keeps the rules and (3) Jesus is punished by God, so humans are now forgiven.

The proper context for understanding Romans 3 is the covenant of vocation, particularly the covenantal understanding of God's work to set right a world gone wrong. Israel's vocation is to be a "light to those who are in darkness" (Romans 2:19) and the promises given to Abraham included that he would "be heir of the world" (Romans

4:13). These two came together in Israel's Messiah. In Jesus, God's faithfulness to Israel and Israel's faithfulness to God has been revealed. The key term underscoring faithfulness to the covenant is the Greek word *dikaiosune* most often translated in English as "righteousness," but best understood as "covenant faithfulness" or "covenant justice." We will return to this important word momentarily.

Not only is the covenant theme necessary to keep in mind as we look at Romans 3:21-26, but so is the idea of worship. In Romans 1, Paul describes the problem of exchanging the worship of Creator for the worship of creation. At the root of sin is a worship problem. Furthermore, the primary object of Jewish sacrificial worship was the Ark of the Covenant, the lid of which is called in Greek *hilasterion*, best translated as "the seat of mercy," "mercy seat," or the "place of atonement." With the themes of covenant and worship from the perspective of the story of Israel fresh in our minds, we are almost ready to dive into this thick text, but first we have to deal with some of the problems we encounter with the typical reading of Romans 3:21-26.

Some readings of Romans jump over large portions of the text to individual verses they piece together to form the "Romans Road," which is straight out of the works contract. "Righteousness" from this perspective is the moral quality of goodness given to us. This definition of righteousness ignores the themes of covenant and worship. Second, the word *hilasterion* is regrettably translated in the ESV as "propitiation," meaning "that which averts divine anger." A further problem occurs when Romans 4 is read understanding Abraham as merely an example of how individuals are justified by faith, ignoring the promises made to Abraham.

The key problem with these readings is they both miss the immediate context established by Romans 2:27-31, namely raising the questions: *Who is a Jew? Who is included in the covenant people of God? What marks people as covenant people?* Paul's argument about who are God's people is built upon Romans 2:17-20 where he reminds the Jews of their vocation to be the light of the world. Paul is not accusing Israel of bigotry. Rather, Israel as the light of the world is supposed to be the answer to the problem, which is not just sinful behavior, but idolatry which has enslaved humanity, hardening people's hearts and causing them to store up wrath "on the day of wrath when God's righteous judgment will be revealed" (Romans 2:5). Nowhere in Romans does Paul talk about the assumed themes of "going to heaven," "getting right with God," or "having a right relationship with God."

The descriptions of divine wrath in Romans 1:18, 2:5-8, 3:5, 4:15, and 5:9 have caused some to wrongly assume *hilasterion* is how divine wrath is dealt with, an assumption made by the ESV in using the word "propitiation." First, the context of covenant and worship causes us to see *hilasterion* referring not to the manner in which wrath is dealt with but to the "mercy seat," the lid to the Ark of the Covenant where blood was sprinkled once a year on the Day of Atonement, where God met with the people of God to cleanse them of their sin. Second, the Jewish sacrificial system makes provision for animal sacrifice but nowhere in the law is the animal offered in place of the worshiper. Third, Paul could have implied that justification in Romans 3:21-26 meant "saved from wrath," but then his statement in Romans 5:9 would not make sense. It would be a logical fallacy, saying the same thing unnecessarily: "being saved by wrath, we shall be saved from wrath." Fourth, Paul mentions that God did not punish sins, but "passed over former sins" (Romans 3:25).

One interpretive key to Romans 3:21 is how we translate the Greek word *dikaiosune* which is most often translated in English as "righteousness." While it has often been understood as a status or quality of moral rightness, it is best understood as "God's faithfulness to the covenant—the covenant not only with Abraham and Israel, but through Israel to the wider world" (Wright, 303). In the Old Testament the word righteousness refers to right things God does, but it is always connected to God doing right things in the light of his fidelity to the covenant with Israel. God did punish Israel as a part of his faithfulness in order to draw Israel back to obedience and faithfulness to the covenant on their part. God's act of punishing his covenant people was not to turn away his anger but to turn Israel back to God's covenant love.

The problem with Israel's faithlessness is that it challenges the faithfulness of God. *How is God going to keep his promises to Abraham if the children of Abraham do not keep up their end of the covenant?* Paul asks the question this way: "What if some were unfaithful? Does their faithlessness nullify the faithfulness of God?" (Romans 3:3). Paul answers, "No way!" God remains faithful. God shows his righteousness, his covenant faithfulness, in the face of Israel's unrighteousness, which is Israel's unfaithfulness. Paul then asks, "Is God unfaithful to inflict wrath on us?" (Romans 3:5). Paul admits he is writing in a "human way." In other words, he is using a human description and attributing it to God as a metaphor. God does not literally inflict wrath, but God does punish his covenant people by giving them up to do what they want, and so they experience the consequences of their actions (Romans 1:28). God's righteousness is not God's moral integrity in a general sense but a very specific faithfulness to the covenant demonstrated in Jesus for bringing justice to the world—setting the world right.

Some fear that this interpretation of Romans 3:21-26 from the perspective of covenant faithfulness will cause people to take sin, punishment, and salvation less seriously, but nothing could be farther from the truth. The reality is the "Romans Road" shortcut which is built upon the works contract is "like a cocktail without the all-important shot of bourbon" (Wright, 307). It has some of the flavors of sin and salvation in it but is missing the real kick of Paul's primary argument. The "Romans Road" misses the story of

Israel altogether. When Paul writes that we have "sinned and fall short of the glory of God" (Romans 3:23), he is using Temple language. The Jewish expectation and longing was for the glory of God, that is God's personal presence, to return to the Temple. Ignoring the story of Israel gives people the wrong impression that God has somehow given up on Israel. Paul's point is that Jews and Gentiles are on equal footing. Israel has shared in the ungodliness of the Gentile pagan world and remains in exile separated from the presence of God.

Jesus is the light of the world as Israel's Messiah. According to Wright, "Incarnation does not cancel election; it brings it to its climax" (Wright, 312). In other words, Jesus does not eliminate the calling of Israel but rather brings the mission of Israel across the finish line. The very definition of God's covenant faithfulness is that God has not abandoned Israel. Romans 3:21-26 deals with the problems of sin and idolatry as well as establishing the ongoing faithfulness of God.

Romans 3:27-31 further grounds the discussion of justification in the context of Jews and Gentiles coming together to worship the one true living God. God's purposes for Israel are fulfilled as God welcomes the Gentiles into God's covenant family in order to rescue the whole world. God offers Jesus as the *hilasterion*, the "mercy seat," as the place where God washed clean the sanctuary that had been polluted by human sin so that God's presence could dwell there. The goal was to restore worship for Israel and for the world, and the means by which worship was to be restored was the covenant.

When we return to look at Romans 3:21-26, we focus on the righteousness of God, the covenant faithfulness of God on display. God's own faithfulness has been made known through the "faithfulness of Jesus Christ" (Romans 3:22). While most English translations render Romans 3:22 "faith in Jesus Christ," the context requires a better translation. If we understand God's righteousness as God's covenant faithfulness we also need to look at how we translate "faith in Jesus." *Is God's covenant faithfulness revealed in our act of believing in Jesus?* It seems like Paul's entire point is leading us to see that God's covenant faithfulness is revealed in what Jesus does, namely his dying. We do experience the benefits of the faithfulness of Jesus in our act of believing in him which is why Paul adds "for all who believe" (Romans 3:22), but God's faithfulness to his covenant is revealed supremely in Jesus' own faithfulness, which includes his death.

God's covenant faithfulness and the covenant membership God offers is a gift of grace. Those who believe and thus put their trust in the faithfulness of Jesus wear faith as a "badge of membership in the new covenant family" (Wright, 320). The death of Jesus does for Israel what Israel could not do—respond to God's faithfulness with faithfulness.

To be "justified by his grace" (Romans 3:24) is to be declared members of Abraham's family and thus in the right. Paul has established that the people of God are no longer marked by circumcision (Romans 2:28-29) and that people will no longer be justified by observing the law (Romans 2:20). A new thing is happening through the death of Jesus. The purposes of Israel are being fulfilled, but the meaning of "Israel" as the covenant people of God will have to be rethought in order to make room for the Gentiles. This justification reveals God's faithfulness, because God is dealing with sin through the death of Jesus. If sin had been ignored God would not have been faithful to the covenant.

Something new has broken in on the earth through the death of Jesus. A revolution has begun and the resurrection of Jesus is the first sign of both the newness and the revolution. The renewed people of God with faith in Jesus have received a verdict in the present that they are in the right (justified), in anticipation of a final judgment that is to come. Those in Christ are no longer under condemnation (Romans 8:1) as sin has already been condemned in Jesus through his death (Romans 8:3).

In Romans 3:24, Paul calls the death of Jesus the *apolytrosis*, or "redemption." The Greek word here is used for redeeming or purchasing a slave from the slave market. This is Exodus language. Israel was enslaved in Egypt, and God redeemed Israel by freeing her from slavery and leading her to the Promised Land. Exodus is the heart of redemption in the story of Israel. The death of Jesus can be viewed as a new Exodus for the new people of God.

In taking a deeper look at *hilasterion*, we turn to look at the instructions for constructing the Ark in Exodus 25:10-22. The lid or covering for the Ark was called "the mercy seat"—Hebrew word *kapporeth*. This covering was not the place where sinners were punished, but a place of meeting. "There I will meet with you, and from above the mercy seat, from between the two cherubim that are on the ark of the testimony..." (Exodus 25:22). In the Greek translation of the Old Testament, the Greek word used for mercy seat is *hilasterion*. When Paul writes of Jesus offering his blood, he uses this Greek word, which has nothing to do with punishment and wrath, but everything to do with worship and cleansing. In Leviticus an animal, the scapegoat, has sins confessed over it, but that animal is not killed as a symbolic act of punishment. Rather it is sent away (Leviticus 16:21). *Hilasterion* is a word drawn from Temple theology, not from pagan religions offering sacrifices to the gods to avert their anger.

God has put forth Jesus not as a propitiatory sacrifice to satisfy God's wrath or honor God's justice. Far from it! For God so loved the world that he gave his Son. God put forth Jesus as the meeting place between God and humanity, where humanity could be cleansed of sin by the taking away of sin. In this way, the death of Jesus shows forth God's covenant faithfulness (Romans 3:25) and demonstrates God's love (Romans 5:8). These themes echo back to the vocation of Israel's servant in Isaiah 40-55. The servant of Isaiah takes upon himself the punishment of Israel, releasing Israel from exile so Israel can be free to carry on with her image-bearing, fruit-producing life. Punishment in this context speaks to the consequences of the nation in disobedience to God. Punishment has a part in the story of redemption, but it cannot outmaneuver what Paul has made central in Romans 3, that is, the never-ending love and covenant faithfulness of God.

Noting the Temple language and Temple theology in Romans 3, we can see that Jesus in his humanity and divinity is the meeting place where God and God's people come together. Indeed heaven and earth have come together in the very place God has chosen to meet with God's people. Jesus' death as described in Romans 3:21-26 further connects with what we have seen in the Gospels. Jesus' death is both a new Exodus and a new Passover. According to Wright, "The death of Jesus was the moment when the great gate of human history, bolted with iron bars and overgrown with toxic weeds, burst open so that the Creator's project of reconciliation between heaven and earth could at last be set in powerful motion" (Wright, 349). In order to follow Wright's interpretation of Romans in a more straight forward, chapter-by-chapter way, check out the Appendix at the end of this reader's guide.

CHAPTER 5 REFLECTION QUESTIONS

1. Where do you see "ungodliness," that is, a lack of proper respect for God in your world?

2. Why is the story of Israel important for understanding what Paul wrote in Romans about the death of Jesus?

3. In the past how have you understood "righteousness"? What does the righteousness of God as "God's covenant faithfulness" mean to you?

4. Why do Christians often assume that someone has to be punished in order for others to be forgiven?

5. Below is one version of the "Romans Road." What is missing from this summary?

    + All have sinned. (Romans 3:23)
    + The wages of sin is death. (Romans 6:23)
    + Christ died for us. (Romans 5:8)
    + Confess with your mouth Jesus is Lord and you shall be saved. (Romans 10:9)

6. In what ways is Jesus our substitute?

7. What does cleansing and taking away sin look like for you?

8. How does Jesus' death become the means for God to set right a world gone wrong?

A REVOLUTIONARY MISSION

The Day the Revolution Began, Chapters 14-15

The earliest Christians, led by the Apostles, understood that with the death of Jesus something had happened; the rumblings of revolution had begun. The first sign that the world was now a very different place was the resurrection of Jesus. The death of Jesus was a decisive victory over the powers of darkness, sin, and death. The kingdom of God had been launched. Since the followers of Jesus believed a revolution had begun, they went forth proclaiming the gospel in the power of suffering love. The question for us modern-day Christians is: *If we believe this revolution continues, then how do we join this kingdom mission?*

Our mission is not simply to tell people about Jesus so they can go to heaven when they die. As we have seen, this becomes a very shrunken view of what the Bible has to say about the goal of salvation. Our mission comes directly out of the triumph and revolution of the cross itself. According to Wright, "Christian mission means implementing the victory that Jesus won on the cross" (Wright, 358). Jesus died certainly as our substitute, but the substitutionary nature of the cross does not take away from the victorious nature of the cross. These two effects of the cross work together. Jesus died in triumph over the powers of evil, and Jesus died as Israel's representative and our substitute in taking away our sins, taking them into death so we could go free. Our mission is both to proclaim and embody this dual meaning of the death of Jesus.

Over the last couple of hundred years, churches and denominations with an evangelical thrust have drifted from an emphasis on cultural and social reform to a mission of "saving souls for heaven." This shift was concurrent with the Enlightenment's secular experiment where all talk of God and religion was slowly but deliberately removed from the public square. Whereas social concerns for public education, care for the poor, and social welfare were once a part of the life of the local church, in these modern days these social needs grew to become a function of the government. In a secular world, religion and the work of the church has become relegated to the work of "spiritual" matters and private moral codes. The way we read Scripture today has been shaped by these cultural influences. In order to see the revolutionary nature of the cross and thus the revolutionary nature of our mission, we need a fresh reading of the Bible in light of its historical context. Wright has worked hard to provide this kind of reading in his book.

Our mission, in part, is to declare the victory of God over the powers of evil, sin, and death, a victory that has the forgiveness of sins at its heart. This victory includes a revolutionary message that challenges the powers ruling our world, making our message inherently political. The proclamation of the forgiveness of sins from the perspective of the Jewish Passover is the proclamation of the end of exile, a liberation from sin that once held us captive which serves as a direct challenge to the principalities and powers. Now freed from sin and the power of evil, we discover a new way of being human in the world. *But what about our personal sins on an individual level?*

Our personal sins need to be pardoned so we can reflect God's image into the world so that the world can be transformed. To be truly human as God designed is to be a "royal priesthood" tending to and caring for the world God loves. We carry out this vocation through our worship, demonstrations of love, and work for justice. We stand as followers of Jesus between heaven and earth. For Wright, "The revolution of the cross sets us free to be in-between people, caught up in the rhythm of worship and mission" (Wright, 363). We also stand at the overlap of ages as people of the age to come where the victory is already won. But we are still living in the present evil age where we fight and struggle against principalities and powers (Ephesians 6:12). We cannot become overly confident in the victory that is won and we cannot live with fear in the face of our present distress. We need rhythm and balance to stay on mission.

Jesus died to save us from the present evil age so that we are free to be the "justified justice-bringers, the reconciled reconcilers, the Passover People" (Wright, 365). Sometimes Christians encounter resistance when working for justice or peace because we have not always been consistent with our message of love. We must own up to our past mistakes, seek forgiveness, and make amends. We shouldn't let the resistance or the guilt we feel from an ugly past deter us from our mission. If we remain faithful to pray through and live out the Sermon on the Mount, we will continue the revolution of the kingdom of God and make the world a better reflection of the glory of God. Our response to the love we see on display at the cross is love of our own, love for God, and love for neighbor. Jesus loved us and gave himself up for us and therefore we must be willing to love and give of ourselves. The world was changed by suffering and dying, and the world will continue to be changed that way.

We are heirs of God and fellow heirs with Jesus if "we suffer with him in order that we may also be glorified with him" (Romans 8:17). Jesus won a great victory by his suffering and we implement Jesus' victory through our willingness to suffer. This kind of mission finds its rootedness in prayer. We confess our willingness to suffer, but we must be careful how we talk about suffering. In some situations, calling the weak or oppressed and marginalized among us to be willing to suffer can come across as unloving and at times unjust. For example, throughout Church history women have been made to suffer unnecessarily. At times their voice and leadership has been silenced by those in authority in the name of "necessary suffering." We must do better.

The Life of Love

The death of Jesus helps us to redefine power from coercion to suffering love. Jesus' victory over the power of domination came through a kind of power rooted in God's covenant love. We live as people of that love demonstrating a new way of being human. This life of love is sustained by the sacramental life of the Church, where through baptism and the celebration of communion we connect with the life, death, and resurrection of Jesus. We die to sin through baptism, dying with Jesus to the old ways of sin and death, and we are raised with Jesus into newness of life. At the table of communion we declare the Lord's death until he comes and share in his broken body and shed blood. The practice of communion declares Jesus' victory over sin, breaking the chains of bondage that had once held us captive. These sacramental acts of worship are at the heart of the Church's mission.

Jesus called his disciples with a simple command, "Follow me." After his resurrection, Jesus sent them on a worldwide mission saying, "Peace be with you. As the Father has sent me, even so I am sending you" (John 20:21). This mission included the proclamation of the revolution that had taken place, a proclamation of repentance and forgiveness of sins (Luke 24:46). The chains of sin that had once enslaved humanity have been broken and something new has broken into our old worn-out world. We need to rethink everything in light of the birth of God's new creation. Forgiveness certainly has personal implications for individuals who repent and believe the good news, but the mission of the early followers of Jesus was bigger than announcing forgiveness to individuals. Forgiveness and liberation have now become the new reality for those who through faith and repentance enter the kingdom of God and participate in God's world-renewing sovereignty.

Faith in Jesus' death and resurrection is a way to say yes to this new reality. While the resurrection of Jesus was the first sign that things are now different after his death, the forgiveness of sins continues to be the sign that God's new creation has taken root. In this new reality, God is restoring human beings to their primary vocation, a new way of being human for those who have only known humanity from the vantage point of sin and idolatry. Forgiveness empowers God's new creation people with a revolution that turns hate into love, bitterness into hope, and sorrow into dancing. Forgiveness and resurrection belong together because forgiveness flows from the defeat of sin and resurrection flows from the defeat of death. Jesus defeated both at the cross.

Jesus sent his disciples to go make disciples of all the nations because the revolution that began with Jesus' death was through

Israel but for the world, freeing the world to worship its Creator. The world's system driven by pride and power, domination and war, has been broken and utterly condemned by Jesus' death. The world's system has been judged and the world's ruler, the satan, has been driven out (John 12:31-32). Within this freedom, the nations of the earth are able to turn away from idolatry and look to King Jesus for the power that gives life.

While the message of the cross was foolishness to many, it was found to carry power by those who believed (1 Corinthians 1:18). The power of the age to come with its love and light has broken into the darkness of the present evil age. With the death of Jesus the powers ruling the world were stripped of their power, and now power itself has to be reimagined. According to Wright, "A revolution has begun, in which power itself is redefined as the power of love" (Wright, 391). The world has a new ruler and he rules not by conventional means of power; Jesus rules by the power of love. We do not invite people to confess faith in Jesus simply so they can go to heaven when they die, but so they can follow Jesus into this revolution of love which shatters the idols of Western culture, the "familiar trio of money, sex, and power" (Wright, 393).

Speaking Truth to the Idols of Money, Sex, and Power

The economic inequality between the global rich and global poor gives us ample evidence that the idol of money is still enslaving people. With militant groups around the world willing to kill in the name of the marginalized and oppressed, we see the seriousness of this form of idolatry. As followers of Jesus we need the gift of discernment to see how the revolutionary cross of Jesus can speak to the economic power brokers of the world. *How can the forgiveness of sins be preached in such a way that the enslaving power of this idol can be broken?* Moreover, those of us who are rich in this present age will need to be honest with what it will cost us to be willing to share with the poor (1 Timothy 6:17-18). We cannot serve two masters. We have to choose between Mammon and the God revealed in Jesus.

The idol of sex is evident all around us—from global human trafficking to the limitless pursuit of sexual pleasure. As the boundaries of sexual norms continue to flex and expand in a growing post-Christian culture, Christians formed by the sexual ethics of Jesus continue to be ridiculed, ignored, and dismissed as socially repressive. It has become nearly impossible to entertain the idea publicly that consenting adults may need to resist acting on certain sexual desires in certain situations. Aphrodite was the goddess of sexual love in the ancient world. *What would it look like for the power of love to confront the power of lust, dethroning Aphrodite?* We followers of Jesus first have to model fidelity to Christian marriage and the historic teachings of the Church regarding sexual ethics. From this position of authenticity and faithfulness we can both offer forgiveness and a call for repentance.

In addition to confronting Mammon and Aphrodite, we must also face Mars, the god of war. Power in our modern world continues to be expressed through violence. The power of love at the heart of the revolutionary cross challenges the uncritical, unquestioning devotion to military solutions to global evil. The victory of Jesus on the cross has broken the forces of evil, dethroning the worship of war, and offering the world a radically new way of addressing conflict. Jesus declares a blessing upon peacemakers as they are in the family business proclaiming a message of forgiveness and reconciliation.

Rejecting the works contract view of rule-keeping does not mean we jettison all practices of morality and Jesus-centered ways of living. Certainly not! However, keeping the rules in the way of revolution is seen as part of the bigger mission to be God's image-bearers on the earth. We willingly share with the poor. We remain faithful to the covenant of marriage. We work for peace. We do so from hearts that have been liberated and formed into the image of Jesus, the perfect image of the Father. In this way, character-based ethics will increasingly look revolutionary in a world where people define themselves by every longing, inclination, and desire of the heart. For Wright, "The gospel Jesus announced was not about getting in touch with your deepest feelings or accepting yourself as you really are. It was about taking up your cross and following him" (Wright, 398).

The power of the cross reveals the emptiness of earthly power, but the function of ruling power is not to be discarded in the Jesus revolution. The story told in Scripture does not encourage anarchy or a world without civil law. Modern democracies have done away with tyrants of the past, but power has shifted to lobby organizations, media outlets, and the wealthy aristocracy, not to mention the military industrial complex. As followers of Jesus in this new creation revolution, we do not merely shrug off political corruption or lobby for a certain candidate who has one or two "Christian" policies as a part of his or her platform. Our role as Passover people, as prophetic people, is to speak truth to power. We are like Jesus before Pilate where we bear witness to another kingdom, a different way to exhibit power, a power enforced by love, not violence.

The revolutionary nature of the cross does not lead us into a non-political pietism. A victory has been won. The powers have been defeated. With the cross before us, we are led into a way of loving that embodies the politics of Jesus. One way we embody Jesus' politics is by our holiness, not according to the works contract, but according to our covenant of vocation. Our holiness is how Jesus is changing the world. Sin keeps the powers in power. We each need to work towards personal holiness, but we must go further. We have a vocation intrinsic to our creation as human beings that goes beyond moral behavior and the assurance of heaven. We have a mission to work with God in God's new creation project, working in the areas of justice and beauty. In this way "holiness and mission are two sides of the same coin" (Wright, 406). They work together in the kingdom of God and the kingdom's work of redeeming the world.

Our mission is not to build the kingdom on earth, but to build *for* the kingdom. Our mission is not about "saving souls for heaven" but about participating with the life of the Spirit in worship and justice as the cruciform people of God on earth. We can say with the Apostle Paul "Christ loved me and gave himself up for me" (Galatians 2:20), but as we have seen, "Christ dying for our sins" is much more than the personal benefits received by each individual believer. We have been forgiven to be co-heirs and co-laborers with Jesus reflecting God's love into God's world.

As we endeavor to love God with all our minds, we continue to wrestle with how early Christians understood the death of Jesus. It is in this work that we worship God with all of our minds, rejecting a Platonized eschatology, moralized anthropology, and a paganized soteriology. These unfortunate theological positions have been replaced with a renewed vision of new creation, our covenant of vocation, and a salvation of love. We embrace them by denying ourselves and taking up the cross, rejecting the temptation to turn our pursuit of the kingdom of God into the pursuit of comfort and "self-realization." We do seek success in following Jesus, but success has been redefined by the revolutionary cross where Jesus died. As Jesus continually demonstrated his love for his disciples, he now commissions us as disciples to be a people of love—loving God, loving neighbors, even loving our enemies.

Our new creation work of love has been made possible through the death of Jesus in that it has broken the power of the satan and empire. Love is how we tell the story of Jesus and love is how we embody the story of Jesus, a love that triumphs over sin and idolatry. We reenact this story in our active participation in worship, particularly in sharing the bread and wine of communion. The cross stands at the center of our faith, the definitive point where the story of God and creation, humanity and Israel, come together into a single tragic point. Through the resurrection we see the revolution that began the day Jesus died. Wright invites us to join Jesus in his new creation, kingdom of God revolution: "Celebrate the revolution that happened once for all when the power of love overcame the love of power. And, in the power of that same love, join in the revolution here and now" (Wright, 416).

I am in. *How about you?*

CHAPTER 6 REFLECTION QUESTIONS

1. If our mission is not to build the kingdom or save souls for heaven, then how would you define the mission of the Church?

2. What does it look like for you to be on mission for God?

3. What does it means to work for peace and justice in your world?

4. Why do so many Christians reject the idea of suffering as a follower of Jesus?

5. Why is the message of forgiveness central to our mission?

6. Which idol is the hardest to critique—money, sex, or power?

7. How does the cross dethrone the god of money (comfort), the god of sex (pleasure), and the god of war (violence)?

8. What steps do you need to take to grow in the power of love?

AN OUTLINE OF THE DEATH OF JESUS IN ROMANS

N.T. Wright's perspective on the death of Jesus in Romans is told in a spiral way with Romans 3:21-26 at the center. In addition to a summary of his spiraling and somewhat complex interpretation of the death of Jesus in Romans, I thought it would be helpful to see Wright's interpretation applied to Romans following Paul's chain of thought. First a couple of opening thoughts:

According to the works contract:

- Romans 1 is how we have broken the rules.
- Romans 2 is mostly ignored.
- Romans 3 is how Jesus was punished for rule-breakers.
- Romans 4 is an example from Abraham's life how individuals are justified by faith.
- Romans 5-8 is about how Christians live out their justification.

According to the Romans Road:

- All have sinned. (Romans 3:23)
- The wages of sin is death. (Romans 6:23)
- Christ died for us. (Romans 5:8)
- Confess Jesus is Lord and you shall be saved and go to heaven. (Romans 10:9)

Both of these approaches miss Paul's point because they have removed the story of Israel. It is also important to note that nowhere in Romans does Paul discuss "going to heaven," "getting right with God," or "having a right relationship with God." Here is a chapter-by-chapter overview of Wright's interpretation with key verses from the ESV included.

Romans 1:1-3: *Paul, a servant of Christ Jesus, called to be an apostle, set apart for the gospel of God, which he promised beforehand through his prophets in the holy Scriptures, concerning his Son, who was descended from David according to the flesh.* The Apostle Paul intends to set forth the beautiful work of God in Christ in the context of the story of Israel. The gospel for which Paul was set apart was the story of Jesus who comes as the grand conclusion to the story of Israel as Jesus is presented here as both God's son and the descendant of the Jewish King David.

Romans 1:16-17: *For I am not ashamed of the gospel, for it is the power of God for salvation to everyone who believes, to the Jew first and also to the Greek. For in it the righteousness of God is revealed from faith for faith, as it is written, "The righteous shall live by faith."* The gospel is for both Jews and Greeks because the great purpose of the gospel is for God to demonstrate his faithfulness to the covenant to bless all the families of the earth through Abraham. The word "righteousness" is the Greek word *dikaiosune*, best understood here as "covenant faithfulness."

Romans 1:18: *For the wrath of God is revealed from heaven against all ungodliness (Greek word asebeia) and unrighteousness of men, who by their unrighteousness suppress the truth. Asebeia,* the lack of proper respect for God, is the problem, not just sinful behavior.

The key passage in Romans 1-4 is 3:21-26, but the context begins in Romans 2: *But because of your hard and impenitent heart you are storing up wrath for yourself on the day of wrath when God's righteous judgment will be revealed* (Romans 2:5). Those who persist in ungodliness and idolatry are enslaved by sin and are storing up wrath, which is judgment to come.

Romans 2:19-21: *But if you call yourself a Jew and rely on the law and boast in God and know his will and approve what is excellent, because you are instructed from the law; and if you are sure that you yourself are a guide to the blind, a light to those who are in darkness....* Paul is not scolding Jews for bigotry or arrogance but he is reminding them of their vocation to be a light to the Gentiles. The people of Israel have failed at their job. They are just as guilty of sin and idolatry as the Gentiles.

Romans 2:27-28: *Then he who is physically uncircumcised but keeps the law will condemn you who have the written code and circumcision but break the law. For no one is a Jew who is merely one outwardly, nor is circumcision outward and physical. But a Jew is one inwardly, and circumcision is a matter of the heart, by the Spirit, not by the letter. His praise is not from man but from God.* Humanity (both Jews and Gentiles) has failed to worship God who is doing a new thing in redefining the people of God without the old Jewish markers.

Romans 3:3: *What if some were unfaithful? Does their faithlessness nullify the faithfulness of God? The problem with Israel's faithlessness is that it challenges the faithfulness of God. How is God going to keep his promises to Abraham if the children of Abraham do not keep up their end of the covenant?* Paul is establishing context here. He is discussing the faithfulness of God.

Romans 3:5: *But if our unrighteousness serves to show the righteousness of God, what shall we say? That God is unrighteous to inflict wrath on us? (I speak in a human way.)* "Wrath" here is not literal anger, but a metaphor drawn from human experience. Wrath is Paul's way of talking about judgement.

God's righteousness is God's covenant faithfulness in Romans 3 based on the context and logical flow of Paul's argument. I've substituted "covenant faithfulness" for righteousness in the Scripture verses below.

Romans 3:21: *But now the* [covenant faithfulness] *of God has been manifested apart from the law, although the Law and the Prophets bear witness to it....* There is a judgment to come (Romans 3:19-20), but now God has revealed his covenant faithfulness in a different way than the way of the written law even though the law and the prophets point to it.

Romans 3:22a: *the* [covenant faithfulness] *of God through* [the faithfulness of] *Jesus Christ for all who believe....* God's covenant faithfulness is revealed through the faithfulness of Jesus and those who believe share in the benefits of Jesus' faithfulness. While most English translations translate verse 22 "faith in Jesus Christ," the context requires a better translation. If we understand God's righteousness as God's covenant faithfulness, then we also need look at how we translate "faith in Jesus." *Is God's covenant faithfulness revealed in our act of believing in Jesus?* It seems like Paul's entire point is leading us to see that God's covenant faithfulness is revealed in Jesus' death. We do experience the benefits of Jesus' faithfulness when we put our faith in Jesus, which is why Paul adds "for all who believe," but God's faithfulness to his covenant is revealed supremely in Jesus' own faithfulness, including his death.

Romans 3:22b-23: *For there is no distinction: for all have sinned and fall short of the glory of God....* The "glory of God" is Temple language. The Jewish expectation and longing was for the glory of God to return to the Temple. Ignoring the story of Israel gives people the wrong impression that God has somehow given up on

Israel. Paul's point is that Jews and Gentiles are on equal footing. Israel has shared in the ungodliness of the Gentile pagan world and remains in exile away from the presence of God. Jews and Gentiles fall short of the experience of God's glory with God's people.

Romans 3:24: ...*and* [Jews and Gentiles] *are justified by his grace as a gift, through the redemption that is in Christ Jesus....* To be justified is to be declared "in the right" by God and thus a member of God's covenant family. All the key theological terms in Romans carry a covenant theme.

Paul calls the death of Jesus the *apolytrosis*, or "redemption." This Greek word is used for redeeming or purchasing a slave from the slave market. This is Exodus language. Israel was enslaved in Egypt and God redeemed them, freeing them from slavery and leading them to the Promised Land. Exodus is the heart of redemption in the story of Israel. The death of Jesus can be viewed as a new Exodus for the new people of God.

Romans 3:25: ...*whom God put forward as a propitiation by his blood, to be received by faith. This was to show God's righteousness, because in his divine forbearance he had passed over former sins.* The Greek word *hilasterion* is regrettably translated in the ESV as "propitiation," meaning "that which averts divine anger." Some have assumed that the death of Jesus is that which propitiates or pacifies the wrath of God, but this assumption does not fit with the story of Israel.

In taking a deeper look at *hilasterion*, we look at the instructions for constructing the Ark in Exodus 25:10-22. The lid or covering for the Ark was called "the mercy seat," Hebrew word *kapporeth*. This covering was not the place where sinners were punished but a place of meeting. In the Greek translation of the Old Testament, the Greek word used for "mercy seat" is *hilasterion*.

When Paul writes of Jesus offering his blood, Paul uses the word *hilasterion*, which has nothing to do with punishment and "wrath" but of worship and cleansing. *Hilasterion* is a word drawn from Temple theology and not pagan religions with sacrifice offered to the gods to avert their anger. "Mercy seat" is a better translation. God put forth Jesus as the meeting place between God and humanity where humanity could be cleansed of sin by the taking away of sin.

Romans 3:26: *It was to show his* [covenant faithfulness] *at the present time, so that he might be just and the justifier of the one who has faith in Jesus.* Faith in Jesus fulfills the law. The law itself finds its culmination in Jesus.

Romans 3:29: *Is God the God of Jews only? Is he not the God of Gentiles also?* Paul has not switched topics. He has tied his argument back into Romans 2:28 and following. Jews and Gentiles have both sinned. Jews and Gentiles are being justified into one family.

Romans 4:11: *Abraham was the father "of all who believe without being circumcised, so that righteousness would be counted to them as well."* The promise to Abraham is that he would be a father of many nations and "heir of the world" (Romans 4:13). Abraham is not merely an example but rather the beginning of God's work of redemption.

Romans 5:1-5 sums up Romans 3:21-4:25. The experience of justification produces a hope rooted in God's love poured into our hearts by the Holy Spirit (Romans 5:5), a love Paul celebrates in Romans 8:31-39 right at the climax of the letter.

Romans 5:9: *Since, therefore, we have now been justified by his blood, much more shall we be saved by him from* [the wrath]. "Wrath" is that which is revealed from heaven against ungodliness (Romans 1:18) and is being stored up by those with stubborn unrepentant hearts (Romans 2:5). Wrath here is a picture of God's eschatological judgment. Most English translations include the words "of God" at the end of verse 9, but the Greek text only says "the wrath," meaning "the judgment."

Romans 5:10: *For if while we were enemies we were reconciled to God by the death of his Son, much more, now that we are reconciled, shall we be saved by his life.* We were reconciled to God by the death of Jesus, even though Paul does not explain exactly how. We were practicing ungodliness, but Jesus' death has freed us to worship the true God.

Romans 5:17: *For if, because of one man's trespass, death reigned through that one man, much more will those who receive the abundance of grace and the free gift of righteousness reign in life through the one man Jesus Christ.* This "reign in life" refers to sharing in the reign of God, which is the kingdom of God. Through the death of Christ, the covenant of vocation is back on track. The free gift of "righteousness" whereby "many will be made righteous" (Romans 5:19) speaks not of our moral standing before God but of our standing within God's covenant family. The gift of righteousness is the "gift of covenant membership."

Romans 6:4: *We were buried therefore with him by baptism into death, in order that, just as Christ was raised from the dead by the glory of the Father, we too might walk in newness of life.* Romans 6 pictures baptism as the means by which we identify with the death of Jesus in order that we may "walk in newness of life." Sin becomes personified as the slavemaster and baptism becomes a picture of the crossing of the Red Sea, where the people of God leave behind the slavery of Egypt for a new life in God's Promised Land.

Romans 6:16: *Do you not know that if you present yourselves to anyone as obedient slaves, you are slaves of the one whom you obey, either of sin, which leads to death, or of obedience, which leads to righteousness?* We were enslaved to sin but Jesus has died to sin, freeing us from the dominion of sin and death. With these words, Paul draws upon the Passover theme and the end of exile through the forgiveness of sins.

Romans 7:4: *Likewise, my brothers, you also have died to the law through the body of Christ, so that you may belong to another, to him who has been raised from the dead, in order that we may bear fruit for*

God. We have died to the law through Jesus' death "in order that we may bear fruit for God," a reference to Jesus' words in John 15:5 and the words of Isaiah in Isaiah 32:16, 45:8. Our covenant of vocation to be image bearers of God is the fruit God is looking for. What Paul described is a new Exodus movement, a kingdom of God movement, and it works because Jesus represents his people. What happened to him happened to us. He died and was raised.

In Christ, we die to sin and are raised to newness of life. Jesus is both our representative and our substitute. Sin with its enslaving power has been defeated. None of this can be reduced to simple formulas or quick and easy summaries outside of "Christ died for our sins in accordance with the Scriptures."

Romans 8:1-3: *There is therefore now no condemnation for those who are in Christ Jesus. For the law of the Spirit of life has set you free in Christ Jesus from the law of sin and death. For God has done what the law, weakened by the flesh, could not do. By sending his own Son in the likeness of sinful flesh and for sin, he condemned sin in the flesh.* God did not punish Jesus. Rather, God punished sin in the body of Jesus. God declares that those in Christ are in the right, in the covenant family (Romans 5:19), and God declares sin condemned. In this way Jesus' death is substitutionary. Sin has been condemned and now there is no condemnation for those in Christ.

This of course is a short summary of some of the themes in Romans regarding the death of Jesus. The major themes of Romans go far beyond what can be summarized here.

ALSO FROM DOCTRINA PRESS

Through the Eyes of N.T. Wright

A Reader's Guide to Paul and the Faithfulness of God
By Derek Vreeland

This helpful reader's guide sums up the primary arguments and conclusions from N.T. Wright by creating a readable roadmap to help you navigate through Wright's big book on Paul's theology.

"The best result of Derek Vreeland's summaries of the magisterial work of N.T. Wright, Paul and the Faithfulness of God, will be when readers read Derek with a view to dipping here and there for long spells in Wright's own book. Wright's book on Paul is very, very long — and probably too long for many who most need it — but the prose is accessible and the insights remarkable so this summary of Paul and the Faithfulness of God will open up the fullness of this new vision of the apostle Paul. I commend Derek's work because I commend Wright's work."

—SCOT MCKNIGHT, Professor of New Testament, Northern Seminary

AVAILABLE NOW ON AMAZON.COM

Printed in Great Britain
by Amazon